THE
DOLLHOUSE
IDEA BOOK

THE DOLLHOUSE IDEA BOOK

Furniture and Decoration

(Previously published as *Dolls' Houses*)

PAULINE FLICK and
VALERIE JACKSON
Illustrated by Ian Douglass

HAWTHORN BOOKS, INC.
Publishers / NEW YORK

Contents

THE DOLLHOUSE IDEA BOOK

A House
to Furnish

A DOLLS' HOUSE used to be something much more than just a child's toy. Many of the earliest ones, made in Germany and Holland in the seventeenth century, were superb marquetry cabinets which opened to reveal a set of Lilliputian panelled rooms, and such sophisticated playthings were clearly intended to amuse grown-ups rather than children, and to grace the drawing-room rather than the nursery. The more elaborate cabinets had fronts inspired by the façades of their wealthy owners' homes, while others had simpler doors like those of an ordinary cupboard; but whatever the outside was like, the little rooms inside were packed with exquisite miniatures representing every possible piece of domestic equipment. Woodworkers, glass-blowers, porcelain manufacturers and above all silversmiths turned out thousands of costly toys to delight adult collectors, and from the fully-furnished dolls' houses on show in various museums—and in particular the Rijksmuseum in Amsterdam—we can see that these enchanting ornaments never suffered the rough-and-tumble of nursery life.

By the beginning of the eighteenth century the continental craze for model houses had spread to England, where baby-houses, as they were then called, took on a more toy-like air. A sturdy oak model, given by Queen Anne to her god-daughter Ann Sharp, can still be seen in the Strangers' Hall Museum at Norwich, with almost all its original furniture and fittings. Like so many toys of this period it

3

was meant to educate as well as amuse, and Ann Sharp would, it was hoped, learn the fundamentals of household management as she arranged the furniture, deployed the servants and mastered the intricacies of the array of domestic gadgets—spits, roasting-jacks, posset-pans, plate-warmers, wine-coolers, candle-snuffers (silver, incidentally, and hallmarked 1686), pestles, mortars and scales; evidently the little Sharps' playtime was closely supervised, or such tiny, vulnerable toys could never have survived for us to marvel at today.

Many other lovely baby-houses were made in England during the eighteenth century, the more elaborate ones still intended primarily for adult amusement. Often they were designed by professional architects, and were every bit as grand, with their tall windows, balconies, coats of arms and roof-top statues, as the real-life classical mansions then springing up all over the country. No description or photograph can do justice to their subtle charm, or convey the quality of the craftsmanship which went into their hand-painted 'Chinese' wallpapers, marble chimney-pieces, steel firegrates, silver candelabra, four-poster beds hung with brocade curtains, folding card-tables and Chippendale chairs. To appreciate the way every detail of Georgian life was lovingly scaled down for these miniature households you simply have to go and look at one; luckily a surprising number has been preserved and can be seen in various public and private collections, with outstanding examples in the Bethnal Green Museum in London, England; and the Overbeck Fantasy Castle in Edwardsville, Illinois. Most collectors are only too willing to show their treasures to anyone genuinely interested, although naturally there are now far fewer eighteenth-century baby-houses in private hands than there are nineteenth-century dolls' houses.

By the late 1700s the fashion for adult-orientated miniatures seems to have been on the wane, and toy-makers were beginning to produce much simpler houses which children could enjoy unsupervised: if the woodwork got damaged,

4

or the furniture was accidentally stepped on or lost, nobody minded much. This more liberal attitude was not confined to dolls' houses, of course; towards the end of the eighteenth century the entire toy trade got an enormous boost from the growing middle-class market and from the new and revolutionary idea that children should occasionally be allowed to enjoy play for its own sake, without any obvious educational overtones. Mass-production was well and truly under way by the time Queen Victoria came to the throne, and all through her long reign huge quantities of intriguing new toys were continually coming on to the market, mostly imported from Germany. The abundance of dolls' house furniture included metal firegrates, rosewood sewing tables, china tea-sets, mounted stags' heads for baronial halls, velvet-upholstered sofas and all the rest of the paraphernalia of the nineteenth-century family residence. Extra pieces were made at home too—wooden furniture by fathers and older brothers, and petit-point carpets, gilt-framed pictures and tiny bed-clothes by indulgent mothers and aunts. Children themselves made little chairs out of conkers and pins, wishbones, or even feathers, and some of these fragile home-made toys are still intact and on display in several museum collections.

With rising labour costs dolls' houses went sadly downhill in the early years of this century. There are a few remarkable exceptions, but by and large they became much flimsier, with rather mean proportions and furnishings to match. Happily the perennial appeal of anything tiny triumphed even over these shortcomings and with an unbroken run of more than 200 years the dolls' house was still as popular as ever as a nursery toy. In the 1920s, however, grown-ups began to realise what they were missing when Queen Mary's fabulous dolls' mansion reminded them how enchanting a real craftsman-made miniature house could be; this model, now on view at Windsor Castle in England, was designed by Lutyens and furnished with pieces specially created to the most exacting standards.

5

Eminent artists painted tiny pictures, M. R. James wrote a ghost story for the library, and a leading jam manufacturer produced minute jars of high-quality preserves for the store-room. Everything is perfectly to scale, and every contemporary luxury, from a Rolls-Royce to genuine vintage wine, has been provided.

Colleen Moore's fairy-tale castle in Chicago's Museum of Science and Industry is another spectacular example of the dolls' house revival in the 1920s. This impressive building weighs about a ton, with castellated towers, running water (distilled, to prevent corrosion of the pipes), a comprehensive electrical system, priceless furniture including a pair of platinum chairs set with emeralds and diamonds and, in the chapel, a reputed fragment of the True Cross. Clearly a model like this is in no sense a child's plaything, but an imaginative *tour de force* demonstrating how one modern enthusiast has reinterpreted the eighteenth-century delight in costly miniatures.

Queen Mary's and Colleen Moore's are two of the most impressive dolls' houses built in the 1920s, though 'dolls' house' is hardly the right word for them since neither edifice contains a single doll. Doll-less too is Titania's Palace, a Renaissance palazzo planned by Sir Nevile Wilkinson as a gift for his young daughter; it was begun in 1907 and took fifteen years to build, and by the time it was finished the little girl had grown up. In any case it was so packed with tiny works of art—statues said to be by Benvenuto Cellini, a jewelled fairy throne, mosaics and a host of other treasures—that it was more suitable for looking at than playing with. Titania's Palace was subsequently exhibited all over the world, and raised huge sums for children's charities.

Few collectors today would want to embark on a project of such magnificence. Quite apart from the prohibitive expense and the question of space, many people prefer the more cosy, domestic type of dolls' house, and the summit of their ambition is to find a dilapidated old Victorian specimen, complete with its original contents, forgotten and mouldering in some dusty attic. It's a lovely dream, but alas most attics and outhouses were cleared out long ago, and period toys have become big business. Usually they change hands through recognised dealers or in the great auction rooms, and bargains are few and far between. Very rarely do eighteenth-century baby-houses come on to the open market, and although Victorian ones are comparatively plentiful in the salerooms they seldom have much of their original furniture left.

Still, the lure of the chase is half the fun of collecting, and one of the delights of owning a dolls' house is that you can go on adding to it ad infinitum. A collection of tiny things neatly arranged in a cupboard-like container also has a lot to recommend it if you live anywhere with limited storage space, as most of us do these days. But the great joy for many enthusiasts is the enormous satisfaction of actually creating miniatures, both for period and modern houses, and it is to these 'makers' that this book is primarily directed.

Both in Britain and the United States there are special clubs and magazines for dolls' house owners, and craft shops geared to their needs. One talented engineer spends his leisure time reproducing perfect Chippendale-style chairs and tallboys, while another collector—a busy housewife—does her best to satisfy her friends' orders for miniature carpet-beaters, clothes-baskets and bird-cages all made from the finest cane. Yet another devises arrangements of wax fruit under glass domes barely an inch high—the very essence of the Victorian parlour.

Wooden dolls' house furniture is still made commercially by several firms, and this will provide the basics for anyone who jibs at carpentry but would like to tackle the more decorative details of furnishing—the floor coverings, wallpapers, pictures and ornaments, which can all be contrived without any special technical skills. Some plastic furniture is amazingly realistic, with proper pull-out drawers and

7

hinged cupboards; being very cheap it is ideal for children to buy and play with, but it has its place too in more 'adult' houses. Although many collectors are inclined to be rather scathing about plastic, it *is* representative of the toys being produced in the 1970s, and deserves attention.

Some enthusiasts start off with an empty house, while others collect furniture first and then look for something to put it in. Naturally it helps to be the proud possessor of a big old dolls' house, but many people begin by making do with a mass-produced modern one or a converted wooden box. Even a cardboard box can be surprisingly strong (wine merchants often throw out very good, rigid cartons) and suitably decorated, these can easily be turned into a set of miniature rooms. This house was made from a butter box picked up outside the grocer's; its two rooms are just the right size for the dolls' furniture being sold today, which usually keeps to a scale of something like 1:16 or 1:12. A house like this could be produced in an evening, and the materials needed would cost almost nothing: glue, paste, oddments of wallpaper, scraps of felt or plastic for floor covering and strips of card or moulding for architectural details like skirting boards and cornices.

A sitting-room, a bedroom and a kitchen would make a good beginning. There is no need for them all to be under the same roof, or enclosed by doors; some experts actually prefer to display their miniatures in separate open-fronted model rooms, so that the detailed interiors get all the prominence, unobscured by an elaborate setting. There is the most delightful set of miniature rooms in the American Museum in Britain (at Claverton, near Bath), based on exactly the same plan as the 'Nuremberg' toy kitchens which go back at least to the 1600s. These early models were really no more than three-sided boxes (or four, counting the floor) crammed with tiny replicas of every conceivable piece of kitchen furniture and equipment.

The kitchen always gives a dolls' house great character. From the domestic quarters of the eighteenth century,

Modern house made from a cardboard box

Traditional farmhouse kitchen

furnished with unfamiliar roasting-spits and chocolate pots, to the kitchenette of a modern 'semi' complete with pop-up toaster and electric mixer, this is the room people always notice first when admiring a dolls' house. An astonishing number of things, like the pop-up toaster and the mixer, can be bought in toyshops and other amusing bits and pieces like plates of food, rugs, storage jars, drying-up cloths, baskets, pot-plants and ornaments can very easily be made at home.

Even if the main pieces of furniture are bought, the other rooms can be made much more interesting by adding home-made bed-clothes, curtains, cushions and carpets, towels with fringed ends—even an embroidered sampler perhaps. Pictures can be cut from magazines or Christmas cards, or painted in water-colours, and then framed in brass curtain rings or strips of balsa wood. Many of the ideas in this book are very simple indeed, and they can easily be copied by any little girl—or boy for that matter, since boys are often

Labour-saving modern kitchen

fascinated by dolls' houses; others are slightly more ambitious, and a grown-up's help would be useful when cutting wood or taking careful measurements. Some, like the elaborate Victorian sofa and the William Morris chair, are really quite complicated and will appeal more to the keen modelmaker.

An old-fashioned farmhouse, a streamlined flat, a home for a Victorian family or the setting for a Jane Austen novel —all these and endless others are possibilities for the dolls' house decorator. Some small, beautifully made teddy bears started us off on a 'Goldilocks and the Three Bears' theme, and the result was an unusual and very well-received dolls' house for a child, fitted out with the requisite number of porridge bowls, patchwork quilts and cottagey chairs.

Anybody catching miniature mania will soon find themselves studying the history of costume and furnishing, poring over the illustrations in Mrs. Beeton's books, and compulsively saving empty matchboxes and the tops from

11

toothpaste tubes because they can be transformed into cupboards and flower pots. All kinds of trivia—small tins, pins with glass heads, brass paper-fasteners, pill bottles and pieces of broken jewellery are suddenly perceived with new eyes as you realise their undoubted possibilities: it is all to do with the delight in smallness for smallness' sake, easy to recognise but impossible to explain. The whole family can share the pleasure of creating a model, and some of the interesting dolls' houses being put together now certainly ought to be passed on as heirlooms. After all, a hundred years from now a toy vacuum cleaner may well be a rare museum piece, and a dolls' house full of the gadgets of the 1970s will become, in time, as strange and fascinating as any of the miniature mansions of the past.

Rush-seated chair inspired
by William Morris

The Tools you Need

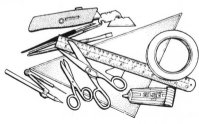

I<small>T REALLY ISN'T</small> necessary to go out and buy special tools for making a dolls' house. Most homes already have them all, tucked away in odd corners. It will save a great deal of time and temper when you actually settle down to work if you gather them together before you start. Keep the tools together in a drawer or a box if possible, where you can get at them easily—or even in a basket.

Cutting and Measuring
No home is without a pair of scissors, but you have to be discriminating about the sort you use. Nail scissors are useless for cutting cardboard or large sheets of paper, and cutting-out scissors are a handicap when negotiating the corners of small designs, so you need two pairs, one small and sharp (the points are sometimes useful for the occasional boring of holes) and one large and sharp. After a spell of heavy duty scissors lose their first fine cutting edge, so a scissors-sharpener (obtainable from most hardware stores) should also have a place in your tool box.

A sharp knife is essential and the most practical way of achieving this is to buy one with changeable blades—you simply replace them when they become blunt. From the many different sorts of craft tool on the market, we recommend the X-Acto knife for its strength, its reasonable price and for the variety of its blades.

13

A fretsaw with blades and a small tenon saw will see you through if you are working with hard wood.

It's a short-sighted policy to cut wire with scissors, so a small pair of wire clippers is a good investment.

A large darning needle set in a cork is a handy tool for scoring paper and boring holes, and a drill has a multitude of uses, among them boring holes and cutting out circular shapes in wood.

Next comes a ruler, a steel one if possible, or one with a steel edge so that you can cut against it. There's a lot to be said for 'going metric', for inches and their fractions have never been precise enough for modelling work, so a ruler with metric measurements will enable you to cut and measure small shapes with great accuracy.

A set square can be added to the ruler, for obtaining true right angles, and compasses for making circles, since one can't always rely on finding something small and circular to draw round when the need arises.

A piece of board to cut on will save table surfaces.

And although it doesn't come under the heading of cutting and measuring, add to your tool box a pair of tweezers for picking up very small bits and pieces.

Smoothing

Sandpaper is essential for a good finish. You can buy it in grades ranging from very rough to very smooth from most hardware stores, but on the small scale on which you will be working only the fine grades are needed. Screen-Bak is an open-meshed cloth used for sanding. It is coated on both sides and can be used dry or wet. Once wet, it can be dried and reused.

Sticking

Though you can buy very small nails with large heads called gimp pins, which can be used when working with wood to reinforce glue joins, most nails are far too big for a dolls' house. On balsa wood or cardboard you can use small

14

dressmakers' pins, but adhesives are essential for most work and it will help if you use one that suits the material you are sticking. In fact, the many excellent adhesives on the market can't do their job properly unless they are used for the right purpose.

Epoxy adhesive is best for heavy-duty sticking, when the two bonded surfaces will be subject to strain, such as on the basic structure of a dolls' house, or on a dolls' house roof that will be lifted off frequently. Epoxy adhesives usually are so strong once they have set that they can never be unstuck, but while they are setting they usually have to be clamped together for about twenty-four hours. However, exceptions to this rule are fast-acting epoxy adhesives that harden like rock in an amazingly short time (five minutes).

Medium-heavy jobs can be done with contact adhesives. A thin film of adhesive is placed on both the surfaces to be stuck together and allowed to dry a little. The surfaces are then joined, when they immediately form such a strong bond that they are hard to separate, so you have to be careful to bring the two surfaces together accurately. This means that contact adhesives are suitable only for certain types of work. You wouldn't use them, for example, to stick dozens of tiny beads to a surface because it would take so long to put the glue on all the separate beads, nor would you use them on two surfaces which had to be manipulated into position, but for the straightforward uncomplicated sticking together of two pieces of wood, most hard plastics or metal, contact glues are very good indeed.

When working on a miniature scale, it's more than likely that some glue will seep from where it is needed to where it isn't, and if that is a probability, use a clear cellulose glue that won't show or stain when it has dried. Clear adhesive, which sets quickly, can be used on paper, cardboard or balsa. Always wipe off any surplus because it forms a film when dry and inhibits the use of stains or varnishes.

There is also a general-purpose glue, Duco which can be

15

used on any porous surface, dries clear, and is non-staining, all of which attributes are an advantage in model making.

A latex adhesive is commonly used to stick fabrics together and you can also obtain a solvent for this in case you drop spots where they are not wanted.

Polystyrene needs its own special adhesive, as contact and clear glues will cause it to disintegrate.

For wallpapering, you could use clear adhesive, like white Elmer's glue, but the best and easiest thing to use is rubber cement, which enables you to slide the paper about until it lands in the right position. It also acts as a sort of glue-size to help strengthen and protect the surface of the paper.

As things often need to be held together while they set, you will find a bulldog clip and some spring clothes pegs, elastic bands, string and wire useful for this. In a class by themselves and indispensable are Scotch tape (this comes in many different varieties including double-sided, which can be used for sticking pictures to walls) gummed papers, and that time-honoured stand-by, needle and thread.

Colouring

Creating a dolls' house involves several skills, among them those of the designer and artist, and for this part, which to some of us is the most satisfying of all, you will need a notebook for planning and rough sketching, sharp pencils, an eraser, and good quality brushes. You can get along with about three brushes, ranging in size from fine to broad, if you keep them in good condition. Rinse them after use in turpentine and then wash them in warm water and detergent, after using them for oil-based paints. Hardened paint brushes can be soaked in commercial paintbrush cleaner, then washed.

Colours of various kinds will be needed to suit the different surfaces upon which you will be working. Felt-tipped pens can be effective and are quick and easy to use on paper and cardboard, but their colours are rather harsh. Subtler shades can be achieved with water-colours, which are transparent but good for delicate work on paper and cardboard. To preserve these colours, which will of course run if they get damp or wet, they can be given a coat of sizing or a coat of watered-down Duco, or they can be varnished when they are dry. To make water-colours opaque so that they can be used on wood, metal or plastic, white gouache, white poster paint or white emulsion paint can be added. (This latter will also make it waterproof.) A tin of white emulsion paint is a useful thing to have by you at all times as it covers well, dries quickly and can be used as an all-purpose undercoat. A good tip, by the way, when trying to paint with a water-based paint on a shiny surface is to mix the paint with a little soap or detergent.

All these white additions will make the colours pale and matt. If you want a gloss finish, varnish over the last coat.

Poster paints are altogether stronger colours, but water-proof them as above and use them on cardboard or paper.

Acrylic colours are stronger in tone and give a long-lasting, waterproof finish. They dry quickly (almost too quickly sometimes), are mixed with water and so can be used thinly as water-colour, or thickly like oil-colour on paper, cardboard, wood, metal or plastic.

You can also use artist's oil-colours on wood, metal and plastic but as they are comparatively slow-drying and as you usually find yourself holding in your fingers the small things you are making, the paint tends to get on you rather than on them, so oil paint isn't really the best medium for this kind of work.

Quick-drying lacquers give a brilliant shiny finish on wood and metal surfaces, and you can buy them in very small tins—so there isn't any waste—from hobby shops.

Coloured inks are useful for fine work on paper.

Add a small tin of clear, quick-drying polyurethane varnish to your paint supply. A coat of it will protect water-colour paint, bring up its colours and impart a gloss, but if you are using varnish directly on paper or cardboard, always glue-size the paper first to prevent the varnish from sinking in unevenly. Two or more coats of varnish also give a good shiny finish to balsa and other woods.

Different wood stains are available if you want a convincing wood finish, though we find that paint plus varnish is just as effective, and cheaper. Cheaper still is brown or black shoe polish, or a mixture of both for an antique effect.

Small pots of gold, silver and copper paint will be useful for making items like coal scuttles, fire irons, mirrors and so on.

When using paints you will need either paint rags or a roll of paper towels for wiping brushes, and you will also need a solvent for all enamel and oil painting.

Graph paper is a godsend at the pattern-making stage as it saves a lot of measuring. Tracing paper too is invaluable when one is designing anything with a complicated symmetrical shape, such as the back of a Victorian sofa or sideboard. Just draw one half, trace it, and reverse for the other half.

Choosing Materials

Wood

IN SPITE OF all the new materials that have been discovered over the past fifty years or so, many of which are extremely useful to the dolls' house enthusiast, wood is still the most popular choice for any sort of permanent structure, with thick cardboard coming a close second. Because wood is such a hard substance, you need fairly sophisticated tools to deal with it and a fair amount of skill to manipulate it. However, properly constructed, a wooden dolls' house or piece of dolls' house furniture will stand up to rough treatment and last for years. Some woods are less intractable than others. Plywood, which is constructed of different layers of wood running at right angles to each other to prevent splitting, can be bought in many different thicknesses, including one so fine that it can be cut with scissors. (This is normally found in hobby shops.) Veneer is another thin wood and this is found in some do-it-yourself shops. It can be used in conjunction with other, softer woods.

It's worth taking a good look round do-it-yourself shops just to see what useful bits you can find—odd ends of wood, small lengths of half-inch and quarter-inch round, square or patterned beading, and round dowelling, all of which can be used for furniture. Off-cuts of plywood or blockboard are other things to track down if you want to construct a house. Have a rough idea of the sizes required

19

before starting to search and then you should be able to buy what you need for next to nothing. Most shops will trim to size.

Never walk past a builder's tip (those huge barrows you sometimes see standing outside empty houses) without peering inside. The uninitiated may consider you a little eccentric as you tweak at the rubble in your best gloves, but you never know your luck—some of our most successful finds have come from tips.

Collect pieces of turned wood such as the bases of chessmen or lace bobbins, as they come in very handy for legs, pedestals, banisters, and finials. Wooden matchboxes are also useful. Soak off the paper covers before using them.

Hardboard

Hardboard is also obtainable from do-it-yourself shops, but it isn't really the ideal material for a dolls' house or for miniature furniture because it is fibrous and heavy, and the rough surface on one of its sides can be difficult to camouflage.

Balsa Wood

Because balsa wood is very soft, carpenter's tools are not needed when working with balsa, but you do need a very sharp knife. Balsa comes in a variety of shapes—flat sheets, square and round lengths, all of different thicknesses, and it can be stuck with clear or contact glue. Balsa wood can't be used to make things that are going to be roughly handled, so it isn't much good for children's toys, but it is a delightful material for creating model rooms. It is porous so needs a proper undercoat but after that it can be treated to resemble any sort of wood you please, or it can be painted. Balsa wood is usually stocked by hobby shops.

Metal

Wire can be bought in many different thicknesses and types from hardware stores, and it has many purposes. Stainless steel wire of suitable thickness can be bent into the shape of tubular furniture, or you could make little wrought iron chairs and beds by curling fuse wire round a pencil to form patterns, then painting it black. Hair pins serve very well if you have no wire. Thick foil (either buy it from hobby shops or use frozen-food containers) can be given a stamped design with a pin for mirrors, lanterns and a host of other things. There are hundreds of uses for pins, particularly brass ones; making bird-cages is one of them.

Plastic

The flat surfaces of polyurethane containers (e.g. detergent bottles) even though tough, are easily cut with a sharp knife to make plastic table-tops, door-facings, bathroom walls or sink tops. Thin stick-on plastic Con-Tact is excellent for kitchen and bathroom floors.

Polystyrene foam (which can be cut with a hot knife or a hot wire-cutter) is an excellent foundation for modern chunky chairs, before covering them with fabric. Use old ceiling tiles or the inside packing from boxes.

Some hobby shops sell thin plastic sheeting which looks much like thin cardboard but is stronger and stiffer and can be used to construct cupboards—or do anything else that cardboard can do.

Plastic foam rubber comes into its own for upholstery, mattresses or other padding, while coarse plastic foam sponge can be painted green and turned into passable trees for the garden.

Cork

Cork is an easily cut, lightweight material which can be used in much the same way as balsa wood.

Cardboard

The great advantages of cardboard are its availability—no house is without its quota of cereal or other packets—and its versatility. If you buy what is known as mounting board in art shops, it is obtainable in various thicknesses from fairly thin to very thick. You can also buy illustration board, mat board and Bristol board, which are all different qualities and have their own sheet thicknesses. The boards purchased in sheet thickness are really laminated papers put together like plywood, round a central core.

Any sort of cardboard can be made stronger by laminating it, that is by cutting several pieces the same size and gluing them together. The finished product is about as strong as wood. Cardboard can also be shaped to make bow-fronted or curved pieces of furniture by first steaming, then bending it to the required form, then holding it in position until it has dried.

Corrugated cardboard is good for fences and roofs. Thin cardboard makes imitation parquet or tile floors. Draw the tiles on first with black ink, then score along the drawn lines and paint and varnish.

All cardboard can be strengthened by the application of sizing and paint. Sturdy cardboard boxes make good temporary houses.

Acetate

Acetate is transparent sheeting which comes in varying thicknesses and looks remarkably like glass. It is suitable for windows, cupboard fronts, glass-topped tables, pictures and the like. You can also buy it coloured for making miniature stained glass! Buy it from art shops or shops specialising in paper, or use old gift boxes.

Paper

Paper is essential for any beautifully finished dolls' house. The pattern on a wall can often make or mar a room.

Collect a lot of different papers. Hoard the end-papers of old books (volumes of sermons are particularly good for marbled papers, which are lovely for bathrooms). Cartridge papers are always a good stand-by for plain walls (or you can paint your own designs on them. Keep colour magazines for their illustrations which will make pictures, murals, clock faces, kitchen details and dozens of other things. Coloured papers will sometimes save you painting.

Hobby shops sell brick, stone-patterned and roof-tile papers, and these are often found in the department for model railway enthusiasts.

Modelling Materials

All kinds of small items can be made with any of the modern substitutes for modelling clay that are available these days, and which do not need high-temperature firing to make them durable. Packaged under different brand names, these clays can be baked in a domestic oven to come out hard and ready to paint. With them you can make ornaments or foods such as jellies, loaves of bread, and everything else for the kitchen, as well as plants for the garden or window box, all at a fraction of the price of models in shops.

If you haven't access to commercial modelling materials, papier mâché is a good substitute. Make it by soaking torn-up paper in water for about twenty-four hours, then draining off the surplus water, first by sieving, then by squeezing with the hands. Make up some wallpaper paste (either flour and water, or cellulose) and mix it into the pulp. As a rough guide, about half a pound of dry torn-up paper will take a dessert-spoonful of cellulose powder—and water, of course. A still quicker method if you need only a small quantity is to mash up a Kleenex tissue and soak that in wallpaper paste. To make a really fine papier mâché, pour a cup of water into an electric blender, add a cup of prepared papier mâché, and mix until finely blended. Then sieve through a fine mesh to get rid of the surplus water. A quick and easy modelling material is made from three parts of flour to one part of salt by volume, mixed into a stiff paste with water. It dries rock hard, either in a slow oven or over a radiator, can be painted and varnished, and will last for years.

Plastic wood can be used for simple modelling jobs. Wrap it round a pipe cleaner when making cabriole legs, for example. Plaster of Paris used with papier mâché produces a very strong mixture, and so does plaster of Paris mixed with water and polyvinyl acetate. Though accurate modelling is difficult with these sticky substances, they can be sandpapered into shape when dry, or used in conjunction with papier mâché.

Fabrics
Don't use synthetic fabrics in an old dolls' house. However superficially suitable they may seem, they never look exactly right *in situ*. Whatever material you choose, make sure it has a small pattern. If fabrics are to drape properly on such a small scale, they must be thin. Thick fabrics produce giant folds that look grotesquely out of proportion in a tiny room. The only possible exception is felt, which is invaluable because it doesn't fray and needs no hemming; it also comes in lovely colours. It makes fine carpets and you can add patterns by painting on it with a felt-nibbed pen or poster paint. Velvet looks especially beautiful in old dolls' houses and is much in keeping since it was used a great deal in Victorian homes, but it does fray badly and can look lumpy unless great care is taken. Lace makes realistic window blinds and, when painted black, spectacular wrought iron for fire screens, balconies or garden chairs. Narrow white-painted lace looks equally well as a plaster cornice for an old room. Ribbons make good

curtains and cushion covers if their patterns are small and pretty. They need to be hemmed along two sides only, or you can stop raw edges from fraying by dabbing them with adhesive. Fur fabric can add an amusing touch of luxury; paint stripes on a beige piece and turn it into a tiger-skin rug.

Always keep a stock of fringes, raffia, cords, lampshade braids, wool, threads and embroidery silks by you. There are dozens of different uses for them. A few scraps of cotton wool should be kept for padding jobs.

Bits and Pieces

No chapter on raw materials would be complete without mention of all the oddments needed to create the minutiae that make a dolls' house so fascinating. To achieve this detail, you need a junk box, a 'bit bag', a button box and a bead box.

Into the junk box can go things like cardboard, small tins, magazines, pieces of wood, matchboxes, cotton reels, cigarette packets, bottle tops, aluminium foil tops, cardboard containers, small plastic boxes, wire, hair grips, metal grommets picked up in the road, nuts and bolts from the tool shed, sea-shells, plastic oddments, tin tacks, washers, curtain rings, collar studs, and all the million and one other things to which only a dolls' house enthusiast would give house-room. One day they will be precisely what you are looking for to give that final touch of perfection to your master-piece.

The 'bit bag' will hold all your scraps of fabric. Have a clear plastic one so that you can see at a glance what it contains.

In the button box keep buttons of every size, shape and description, from cast-off dresses and coats, from jumble sales, from shops and from your friends. They make fine lamp bases, table and stool tops, picture frames, plates, and lots of other things.

The bead box will hold discarded junk jewellery. Earrings are often particularly imaginative—we once found what became two miniature bird-cages in a pile of junk jewellery at a jumble sale. Save embroidery beads, sequins, plastic necklaces, buckles and brooches, and especially glass beads which can be wired together to make crystal chandeliers. Try to separate the beads into colours, sizes and types. Store them in glass jars, otherwise you will have a long search for the right one.

The following chapter gives you ideas on how to use these bits and pieces.

Making Simple Furniture

The Period Dolls' House

WITH RAW MATERIALS and tools assembled, the work of actually making things can start. There's no need to be too ambitious to begin with, since the most delightful results can be achieved with very simple shapes. The important point to remember is scale, so that individual objects relate to each other and to their setting in a satisfactory way. Apart from this, general considerations of style, period, colour and texture apply to dolls' house furnishing just as they do to our own homes.

To get a few ideas it will probably help to take a quick look at the miniature furniture produced over the past 300 years or so. Few amateurs could hope to copy the exquisite pieces in the early baby-houses, where every tiny bed, chest of drawers and cabriole-legged chair is virtually an original work of a master craftsman. It would be even more difficult —in fact quite impossible—to copy modern plastic toy furniture at home: nobody in their senses would want to anyway, when it can be bought so easily and cheaply. But the mass-produced items of, say, 150 years ago are altogether a different kettle of fish; a close inspection reveals that they are often based on very simple structural techniques and rely for their effect on clever surface detail. Even the lovely little simulated rosewood pieces of the mid-nineteenth century, which Mrs. Graham Greene calls 'dolls' Duncan Phyfe' in deference to the celebrated American designer, turn out to be quite simple when one analyses their various component parts.

27

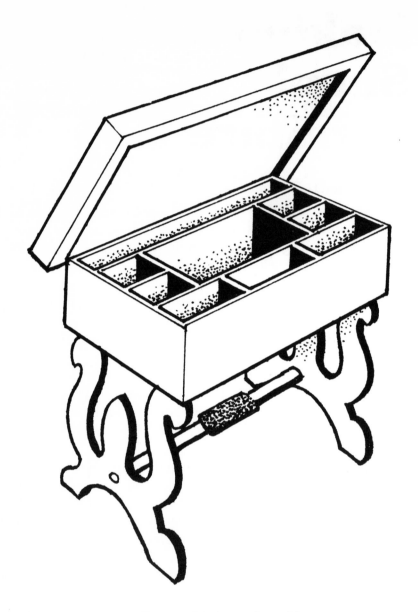

'Duncan Phyfe' sewing table

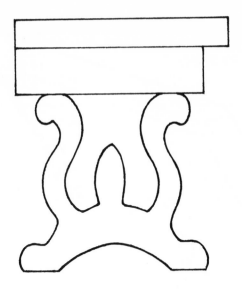

Diagram for copying the sewing table

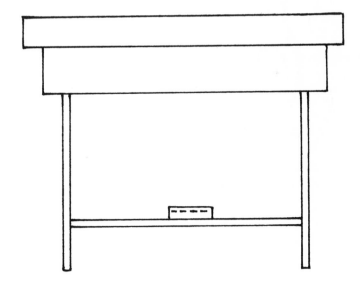

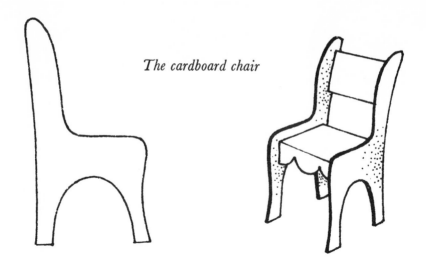

The cardboard chair

Paper and cardboard furniture for dolls has a long history and there is no need to use wood to make authentic-looking period chairs, tables, sofas and washstands. This little cardboard chair in fact dates from the 1930s, but the same sort of basic construction method has been used by generations of toy-makers. Essentially all furniture of this kind consists of two identical profiles, joined together with one or more sandwiched-in pieces. This chair, for example, has two parallel sides, with seat and back glued into position between them. Exactly the same method can be applied to the sabre-legged Regency chair, although naturally the cutting out of this more delicate shape needs more care than the chunky 1930s outline did; also the twin profiles are slightly splayed, making the seat wider at the front than the back, but this adjustment does not present any great difficulties. What 'makes' the Regency chair are the decorative details—the fine striped upholstery, the tiny frieze running along the front of the seat and the decorated back.

The same 'two sides and a middle' method was used for the country rocking-chair; this can be varied by covering the cardboard sections with fabric and oversewing them

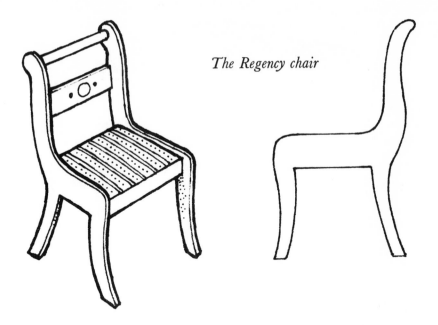

The Regency chair

The rocking chair

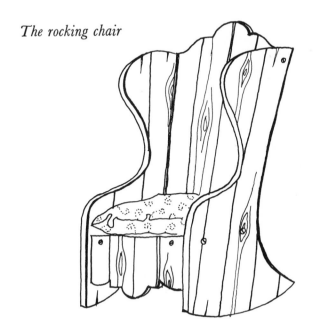

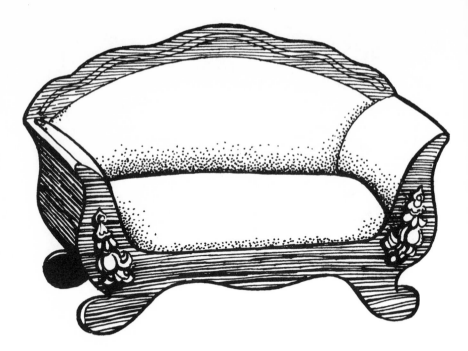

Victorian sofa

together to make a winged armchair (omit the rockers in this case).

The opulent-looking sofa was based on similar ones which we had noticed and admired in many old dolls' houses. Here the profile components are the front and back, with seat and arms sandwiched between them. This model turns out successfully with either a wood or cardboard frame, and wadding or plastic foam will provide the padding for arms, seat and back. The serpentine curve on the outside of the arm-pieces is quite easy to copy if you have a small piece of wood veneer, or use stiffish cartridge paper if you are working in cardboard. Alternatively you can ignore this refinement and have straight sides, as many Victorian toy sofas have. Once again it is the finishing

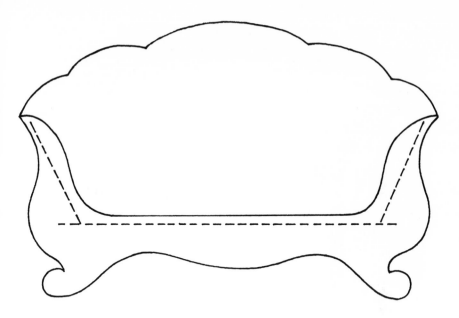

Framework for the sofa

touches which make all the difference—an appropriate silk or mellow brocade for the upholstery, the right choice of gilt appliqués for 'ormolu' mounts (try cut-outs from a gold paper doily if nothing suitable in metal presents itself) and perhaps a bolster-shaped, tasselled cushion.

The sofa technique can be adapted for a variety of chaises-longues (omit the high back and one arm altogether), sleigh-beds and cradles. There is an adorable little couch in the Doll Museum at Warwick, England, with a border of tiny shells running around the back and along the front; uncomfortable though this decoration would be in real life, it is very effective on a toy and the Victorians embellished a lot of their miniature furniture in this way.

Basic table

Dolls' house tables come in all shapes and sizes, with working gate-leg models at either end of the scale: one finds hand-made versions of them in museum baby-houses, and perfectly proportioned modern reproductions in plastic! As always, the amateur will be happiest looking for inspiration mid-way between these extremes, working on simple shapes in wood and cardboard. A plain rectangular table is very easy, being just a top with four straight square legs glued on. What gives it a 'real' look is remembering to set the legs in from the edge, leaving a slight overhang, and running a thin strip of frieze round the top where the legs meet the upper part. This makes a good dining table just as it is, while a stick-on plastic cover will convert it into a kitchen table. It will look modern if it is painted white or matt black, old if it is stained dark brown, or cottagey-trendy if wood the colour of stripped pine is chosen. Use the cover of a small candy tin for the table top and you have a convincing enamel work surface. Reduce the height for a coffee table, or add a foot-rail for a refectory table, with round wooden beads wired together to make those bulbous Jacobean legs. Put drawers in the frieze and stick an oblong of leather on the top and you have a writing table. Experiment with round, oval or square tops as well as oblong; a semi-circular top makes a console table for a hall, or, with muslin drapery, becomes a dressing table.

Antique four-poster beds need no carpentry at all, as their cardboard framework can be completely hidden under curtains and frills. Pencils or lengths of dowelling make adequate bed-posts for a four-poster, though if the bottom two posts are to be exposed something tapering or turned would be prettier—try paint-brush handles (artists', needless to say, not decorators').

The toy half-testers of the Victorian period are particularly endearing, and ideally they ought to be copied in wood to give the characteristic look of solidity. However, in *The Girls' Own Toymaker*, a children's book of the 1860s, instructions were given for half-testers in paper and cardboard. Directions and diagrams both tend to be scanty, and a child was evidently expected to show a good deal of initiative in interpreting them, but the optimistic drawings of the finished objects are so inspiring that we have decided to include one here.

Illustration from The Girl's Own Toymaker, *1860*

Having disposed of chairs, tables, sofas and beds, nearly all the other basic pieces of period dolls' house furniture fall into the 'cupboard' family, which includes anything from a meat-safe to a wardrobe. The essential pieces are two identical parallel sides, joined together with top, bottom, and back pieces. (Make sure that the back always fits *inside* the side sections rather than projecting beyond them, otherwise the finished piece will not stand neatly against a wall.)

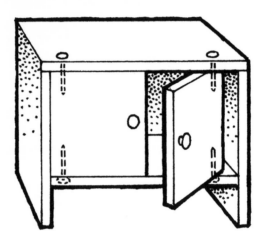

How to hinge a door using two gimp pins

Doors ought always to open, and a comparatively easy way to 'hinge' them is to tap a gimp pin (a small fine nail used by upholsterers) through the top and bottom section and into the door. Provided these pins are exactly in line one above the other the door will open and close most satisfactorily, and all the 'Duncan Phyfe' pieces we have examined seem to rely on this method.

This then is the basic cupboard suitable, say, for a kitchen. But raise it up a little by elongating the sides, add a tiled back, and it becomes a washstand. The one in the illustration was made from cigar box wood (which is a nice colour, but splits easily), and the only cutting tools used were a small hacksaw and an X-Acto knife. It looks professional because each separate section was painstakingly sandpapered, and we cannot over-emphasise the importance of this. When anything is reduced to this scale any roughness or lack of finish sticks out like the proverbial sore thumb, and whether you are working in wood or cardboard meticulous rubbing-down is absolutely essential.

Washstand with a tiled back

37

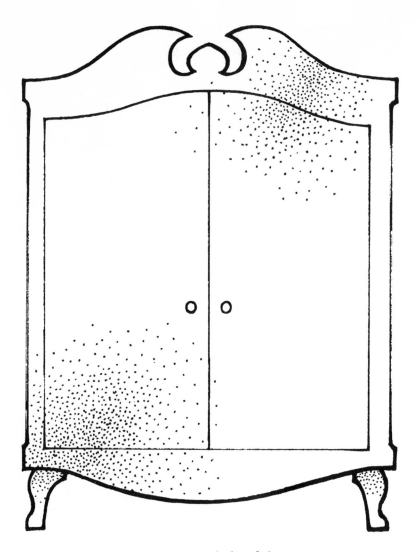

A dolls' house wardrobe of the 1930s

Omit the doors and substitute shelves and the result is a bookcase; in a period setting the shelves could have a scalloped 'leather' edging. Make the cupboard taller, with double doors, and it becomes a wardrobe. These two drawings show a wardrobe from a dolls' reproduction Queen Anne bedroom suite (made in the 1930s) and a Victorian

Wardrobe from a Victorian dolls' house

model of the 'Duncan Phyfe' variety; this one is covered
with printed paper imitating marquetry, which gives it a
very rich look, although the basic shape is quite simple,
being built up entirely of rectangles with no curves at all.
It opens to reveal a row of pegs, while the Queen Anne one
has coat hangers on a minute brass rail.

39

Mahogany sideboard circa *1860*

Other cupboard variations are the little 1860-ish side-board with ornamental back, and a dresser with cupboards below and shelves above. Pins tapped into the front of the shelves will make tiny cup handles. A display cabinet is no more than our old friend the basic cupboard, with a glass door; make a wooden frame to hold the glass pane, but as this is in fact just glued on to the back of the frame its exact dimensions are not critical—a comforting thought, as glass-cutting is a decided knack. There should be shelves inside the cabinet, and an Adam green interior makes an effective background for tiny ornaments.

Some old dolls' houses have built-in fireplaces, with chimney breasts reaching right up to the ceiling, leaving an alcove on either side. A length of plank or a shallow cardboard box will make the chimney projection, which should, of course, be decorated to match the rest of the room. The fireplace, with its surround and mantelshelf, fits in to the opening underneath. This drawing shows a little grate, probably eighteenth-century, found in one old house. The original was made of metal, but to simplify things we copied ours in cardboard, with matchstick bars, finishing it off with several coats of shiny black enamel. The same method can be adapted for other styles of grate, or for a kitchen range, with oven doors drawn on in grey paint and a brass paper-fastener handle. A rough wooden beam topping

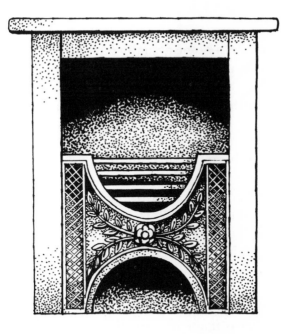

Metal Regency fireplace—copy in wood or cardboard

41

brick or stone uprights will make an inglenook fireplace; add a pile of logs at floor level, and a sprinkling of genuine ash for realism. Swags and rosettes stuck to a plain wood surround will produce something 'after Adam', while decorated tiles cut from magazines or catalogues will give a hearth a *fin de siècle* look.

So much for the basic items for a period dolls' house. The next chapters will deal with the various accessories which make furnishing a model room so absorbing, but in the meantime here are some suggestions for completely modern furniture. Once again the pieces have been chosen to provide the bare bones—fireplaces, chairs, sofa, chests of drawers and beds—and some fresh construction methods have been described in more detail which we hope will suggest many effective ways of using the new materials like polystyrene, cellulose filler and plastic foam which are now available to model-makers.

Modern Furniture

Not every modern home actually has one now that so many rely instead on central heating, but there is no doubt that a fireplace gives a room a focal point that would otherwise have to be invented, or that some up-to-date examples are very attractive indeed, varying in style from the futuristic to the Tudor-traditional.

The only criteria for making a fireplace for a modern dolls' house are that it should harmonise with the room in which it is to go and look as though it could work in real life. Here we show you how to make an ultra-modern free-standing fireplace with a 'brass' hood and a more traditional brick grate, either of which can be adapted according to available materials.

Free-standing Fireplace

The fire basket is made of a small styrofoam ball about $1\frac{1}{2}$ inches in diameter, cut in half (or you could use a ping-pong ball). Scoop the centre out of one half of the ball, and

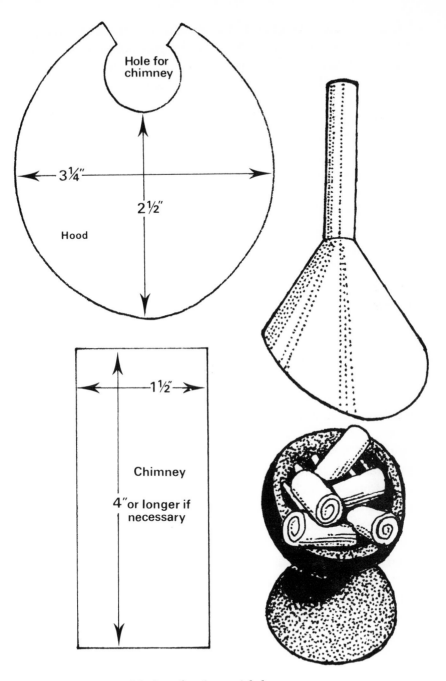

Hole for
chimney

← 3¼" →

2½"

Hood

←1½"→

Chimney

4" or longer if
necessary

Modern fireplace with brass canopy

stick it, hollow side up, on to the other half of the ball, which is left intact, but with its cut side facing down. Cut a dip in the front of the hollow ball, so it looks as though it is sloping upwards towards the back. This is now the fire basket. Coat both halves with a mixture of plaster of Paris and polyvinyl acetate for extra strength. Paint them black and then varnish them to get an iron effect. Stick black-painted toothpicks across the top of the fire basket to form a grid and make some logs out of circular dowelling painted realistically, or pile a few real twigs and small bits of coal on the grid. Strips of rolled, gummed paper also make good logs.

Red crêpe paper or red aluminium foil will help to give a fiery impression. Cut the hood for the fire out of cardboard as shown in the pattern and cover and line it with gold foil paper, sticking with strong adhesive. Cut the chimney section from thick paper as cardboard will not bend successfully on such a small scale. Stick it round a pencil and when the glue has set, remove the pencil. Cover with gold foil, and stick to the hood. Prick nail marks all the way up the chimney. The hood part is attached to the ceiling of the room in which it is to go.

Brick Fireplace
Take a large matchbox, or any cardboard box about 4½ inches high, 2½ inches wide and 1½ inches deep. This will give you a fireplace which would in real life be about 72 inches high and 40 inches wide, working on the 1:16 scale.

Cut a rectangular aperture 1½ inches high by 2¼ inches wide in the front of the box and about 1 inch up from what will be the bottom of the fireplace. This is the basic structure to which can be added, on either side, the tops of two matchboxes to form fireside seats.

Now you need a base for the grate, which will project at the front and act as a fender. Take a piece of card the same width as the aperture you have cut, and bend and score it

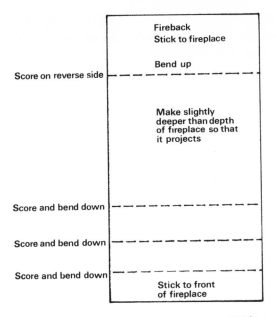

Fireback
Stick to fireplace

Bend up

Score on reverse side

Make slightly
deeper than depth
of fireplace so that
it projects

Score and bend down

Score and bend down

Score and bend down

Stick to front
of fireplace

Brick fireplace with lineback

as shown in the diagram. Precise measurements are not given here, because they will depend on the size of the box you are using, but this plan for bending and scoring will provide a fireback to stick to the back of the aperture, and a projecting fender.

Paint the firebase black and stick the fireback to the back of the fireplace. Add a heraldic fireback made out of black-painted lace or a piece of old buckle or belt. Don't stick the front of the fender down yet—first cover the whole of the fireplace with brick paper (including the seats) and then stick the projecting fender down in front of the fireplace aperture. A piece of black plastic or wire mesh added to the front of the fender will stop the cinders falling out.

The mantelpiece can be made of a strip of balsa wood painted and varnished. A log basket formed by sewing together circles of string, some logs, and a small picture framed in balsa wood, complete the scene.

Chair and Sofa

Modern chairs are being produced in exciting designs which can be easily imitated on a small scale in polystyrene foam or synthetic sponge, cotton wool and cardboard, or almost any other suitable materials. The most difficult part is the covering, because fabric edges fray and delicate materials mark very quickly. This means that even though you can use a solvent to remove the worst of the spilt spots of adhesive, you do have to go very carefully. Felt is one of the best fabrics for upholstery work.

We used toothpaste boxes for the bases of our chair and sofa, and padded them with thin plastic foam. The diagrams show how to cut the boxes to get the required shape. If a box is too long for a sofa, cut out a section and rejoin the ends with Scotch tape.

To cover the chair and sofa, cut three pieces of fabric.

1. Top to front of the chair plus overlap.
2. Outside of arms and overlap.
3. Back and base, no overlap needed.

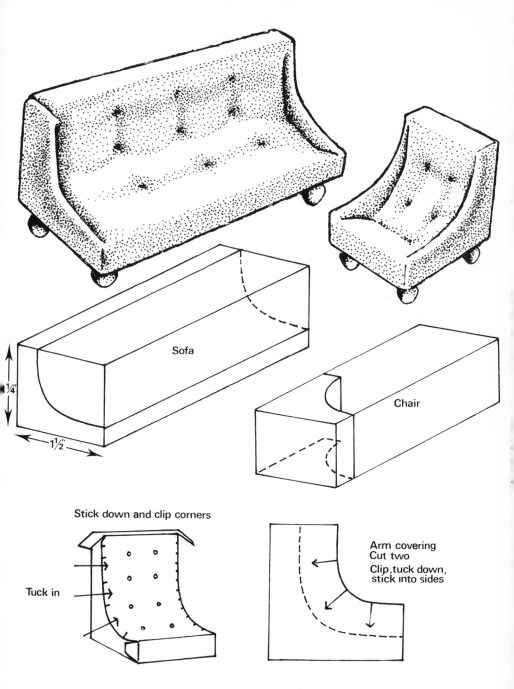

Sofa

¼"

1½"

Chair

Stick down and clip corners

Tuck in

Arm covering
Cut two

Clip, tuck down,
stick into sides

Sofa and chair made out of toothpaste boxes

For the top to front of the chair, cut to allow about $\frac{1}{8}$ inch overlap at both sides and a little bit extra at the top and bottom. Stick the fabric over the front of the seat with fabric adhesive and clip the corners and sides with scissors. Now 'button' the back and seat by stitching right through the chair from back to front, at evenly pre-marked points. Tuck and stick down the side overlaps inside the arms, but stick the top and front overlaps as shown in the diagram.

Now cut two pieces to cover the outside of the arms, clipping where shown, folding over the arms and tucking and sticking down alongside the previously stuck section. Push the sides together to stick tucks in place and to hide the clips, adding extra glue if necessary. Stick the fabric over back and base. Cut four little holes in the felt at the base of the chair and sofa and stick four feet (made from buttons, beads or dowelling) on to the cardboard base.

Chest of Drawers
Though it is quite possible to take short cuts when making a chest of drawers (you could use matchboxes as drawers, for example, and build a frame to fit them), we decided to start from scratch and build a balsa wood chest with three drawers. Ours is 3 inches high, 2 inches wide, and $1\frac{1}{2}$ inches deep, which worked out quite conveniently mathematically, when used with quarter-inch wide balsa strip, as you can see in the diagram.

Cut two pieces of balsa wood $1\frac{1}{2}$ inches $\times$ 3 inches for the sides.

Cut one piece $1\frac{1}{2}$ inches $\times$ 2 inches for the top.

Cut one piece 2 inches $\times$ 3 inches for the back.

These three pieces are stuck together to make the basic frame, which is supported with quarter-inch balsa wood strip battens round the base, as shown in the diagram.

Stick two more sets of battens at $\frac{3}{4}$-inch intervals to act as drawer supports. The three drawers are all $\frac{3}{4}$ inch high, $1\frac{1}{2}$ inches deep and almost 2 inches wide (the difference in width being the thickness of the balsa frame itself).

48

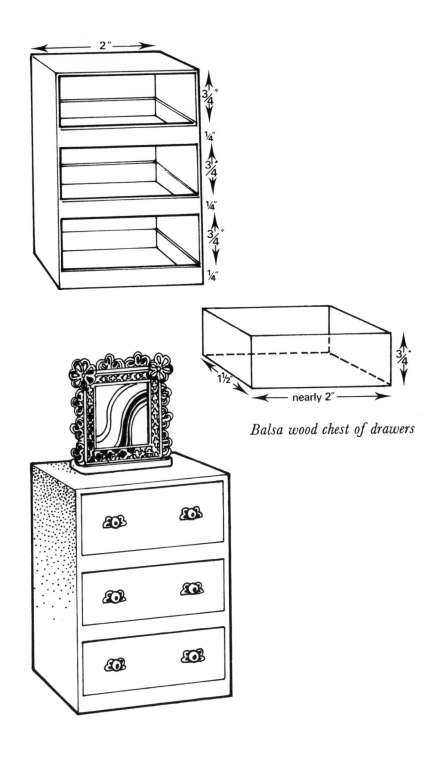

2"

3¾"

¼"

3¼"

¼"

3¼"

¼"

3¼"

1½"

nearly 2"

Balsa wood chest of drawers

When the chest is assembled, give it two or three coats of emulsion paint, sandpapering between each one, and then give a final coat of gloss.

We put bead handles, set on gold paper bases, on our chest, but you could vary things by painting it a different colour, or staining the wood, and adding brass paper-fastener handles, or wooden ones made of small lengths of matchstick.

To make a decorative mirror to go on top, stick a piece of aluminium foil on a cardboard square, and stand it on a small piece of plastic. A decorative gold paper frame gives an exotic, rather Spanish, effect and matches the drawer handles.

Screen

A colourful and imaginative screen placed carefully in a dolls' house can add a touch of intimacy to a sitting room or bedroom. Either use a thick piece of cardboard or laminate two thin pieces of cardboard together and cut out three panels, each one 3 inches × 1½ inches. Hinge the panels by sticking two narrow pieces of ribbon on to two sections, then turning these over, and sticking another piece of ribbon to the third panel and the centre section. Cover the screen on both sides with small-patterned paper, or with cut-out pictures or small paper scraps. Paint the edges of the screen black. Size and then varnish the screen with clear varnish. To make it look old, rub a little burnt umber paint on it, allow to dry, and then varnish.

Bed

These instructions are for a single bed, which in real life would measure about 6 feet long by 2½ feet wide. This works out at 4½ inches long and about 2 inches wide on the 1 : 16 scale. To make a double bed, widen the whole thing.

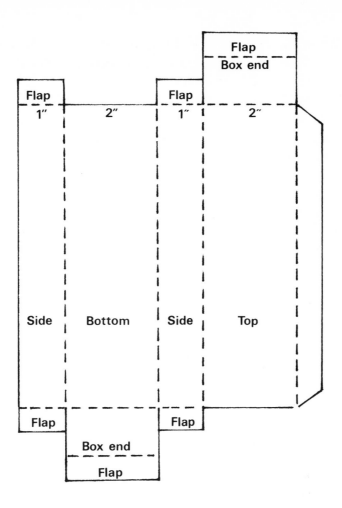

Box base for bed—score and bend along dotted lines and stick down flaps

Take a box the right size, or make a box out of cardboard, as shown in the diagram, scoring along the lines to make for easy folding. This box is 1 inch thick, but if you want a flatter base, make the side sections ½ inch wide. Stick down all flaps securely.

Cut four holes in the bottom of the box at the corners and insert four round dowelling legs, which should be about $1\frac{1}{2}$ inches long. Push the legs through the top of the box and stick them. Make sure the legs are all even in length, sanding the feet level if they are not.

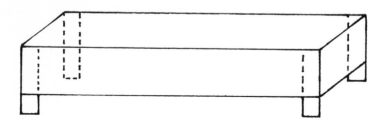

Putting the legs in the bed base. Alternatively, stick beads on base for feet

Cover the bed base with suitable material. You can then make a foam mattress to go on top of the bed base if you like, but we found that too many extras on the bed made it bulky. Instead we covered the base in white sheeting, so that it plays the part of a bottom sheet, made a foam pillow in a white pillow case (with proper turned-in ends), a white top sheet, a red woollen fabric blanket and a frilled, flowered bed cover. We hemmed the sheet by sticking the edges, using a very small amount of adhesive, and we bound the top and bottom of the red blanket with red ribbon, which made it look like an expensive, real blanket. Other finishing touches could be a patchwork quilt (paint a white sheet with patchwork pattern in fabric dye), and a small eiderdown, though these tend to be a bit hard and inflexible when they are padded and quilted. You could also paint patterns on the sheets and pillow cases with fabric dyes, which would look very pretty. By the way, remember to shape the foam pillow by cutting it. Pillows simply are *not* square!

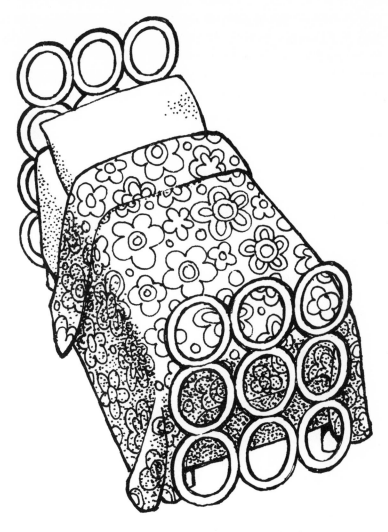

Brass bedstead made from curtain rings

The head and foot of the bed lend themselves to a variety of design. You could pad and button them, make matchstick railings, or paint lace black to represent wrought iron, or make fancy railings from carved balsa wood.

We settled for a brass bedstead made out of small brass curtain rings, stuck together with epoxy glue. When sticking the rings, lay them flat on a piece of cellophane paper and put another sheet of cellophane on top. Put a weight on them and leave them for twenty-four hours. You can then peel off the cellophane without leaving any of it behind. Two strips of balsa wood run underneath the bed base, and are stuck to the curtain ring foot and head, forming a sort of bed frame.

Getting Down to Detail

DOLLS' HOUSES are never finished, and as we've already noticed this is one of the secrets of their fascination. Once the basic furniture has been provided, more and more details can be added, introducing those personal touches which make the rooms look really lived in.

For anybody who does not feel equal to making all the main items, the obvious places to look for dolls' house furniture are toy shops and the toy departments of large stores; novelty shops and stationers in unfashionable side streets often turn out to have a surprising stock, too. Amongst the traditional wooden pieces it is still possible to find dark oak Jacobean-style dining-room suites, beautifully-finished kitchen dressers, grand pianos and drop-side cots, and even the keenest makers will be tempted to buy outstanding models like these.

One dealer's range of plastic furniture included a secretaire desk six inches high, with everything opening and shutting as it should, right down to the pull-out supports for the front flap. (This furniture is no longer produced because of the shortage of raw materials and so these pieces have already become something of collectors' items.) Some plastic pieces are rather spoiled by their colour, but they can be painted quite successfully.

It pays to look round toy shops fairly regularly, as new designs are always being added. Addicts are strongly advised to snap things up just when they see them, as delay can be fatal: production of favourite lines is apt to cease without warning, as in the case of the three flying ducks which graced so many walls in the 1930s; quite recently they were reproduced in miniature, but disappointed collectors report that these delectable ornaments are already unobtainable. However, there is still a good selection of bric-à-brac to be found including a delightful plastic fifty-six-piece dinner and tea service, complete with silver candelabra, knives, forks and spoons and tiny champagne glasses. One miniaturist makes bird-cages, telephones, carpet-sweepers, plate racks, electric fires, ironing boards and a host of other accessories. There are dogs in kennels and cats in baskets especially for dolls' houses, while the farmyard animal counter will provide cows, lambs, hens and ducks to sound a rural note outside.

But the most imaginative toy manufacturers won't have thought of everything, so the answer is to make some of the accessories yourself. Here are some ideas which we hope will help to spark off more of your own.

Food. A dolls' house kitchen looks so much more homely with some food standing about. There are plenty of miniature delicacies in toy shops, but similar dishes are simple to make at home from almost any modelling material. Copy things which are easy to recognise—iced cakes, blancmanges, vegetables, fruit, fish, loaves of bread—and after painting them realistically add a coat of varnish, which will make everything look more appetising, as well as protecting the colours. Either mould a plate in one with the food, or stand it on a suitable dish; stick a pile of fruit on a decorative glass button, for example, or put a cake in a tin sweet-mould. Tin can be painted to look like copper, and shiny foil will make a good metal dish. If inspiration flags turn to Beatrix Potter's illustrations for *The Tale of Two Bad Mice*: who can forget the important part played by the plaster ham and the inedible lobsters in this much-loved story? The pictures in Mrs. Beeton's cookery books are useful too, especially when you are tackling something exotic

Illustration from The Englishwoman's
Cookery Book *by Mrs. Isabella Beeton*

like a decorated boar's head (a surprisingly easy thing to
make, in fact, using a plastic toy pig's head as a base).
Always be on the look-out in sweetshops for any suitable
oddments, and invest in a packet of wine gums for a supply
of ready-made miniature fruit jellies.

Make packets and canisters to stand about on shelves;
use pieces of balsa wood or short lengths of batten or
dowelling, covering them with bright wrappings and làbels
cut from small magazine advertisements. If you have a
fridge which opens, add a few items for this—things like
pats of butter, a bottle of milk with a foil cap, eggs, bacon
and sausages.

An old-fashioned kitchen could have sides of bacon
hanging from the rafters, or strings of onions (small wooden
beads strung together with thin strands of raffia).

Real dry goods from the store cupboard, such as lentils,
hundreds-and-thousands, mustard seeds or sugar, can be put
into little glass or plastic pill jars to look like biscuits, dried
fruit and so on.

More Kitchen Accessories. All kinds of baskets can be made
from coarse string, sewn into a round shape with a single

57

strand of the same string or with raffia. Long grasses can be plaited into lovely baskets, but dampen them first to make them pliable; then plait or twist them into lengths and sew to the required shape with self-coloured cotton. Besides shopping baskets and clothes' baskets for the kitchen we've made an Ali-Baba type linen basket for the bathroom, a sewing basket and a waste-paper basket for the sitting-room and a little plaited cradle for the baby's room.

Thick hollow straw, which makes nice bamboo furniture and wall panelling, can also be used for many other things. If you use barley straw, cut off the golden whiskers and glue and bind them with cotton to a small straight stick to make an old-fashioned besom, or sweeping brush. For the lazy among us, a good tip is to shorten the handle and bristles of a mascara brush to form a small hand brush.

Try to load all the kitchen shelves with food, pots and pans and crockery. Recipe books, a clock and a rolling pin will help to fill any gaps. A charming hen-on-nest dish can be contrived from the upper part of a plastic toy hen sitting on a bowl either moulded from modelling compound or carved out of balsa wood. Top and bottom should be painted to harmonise with each other, and then varnished.

Real-life chopping boards are very decorative these days and few things are simpler to scale down for a dolls' house. Use balsa, thin plywood or stiff card, add a bright design for a splash of colour, and hang it on the wall.

One talented enthusiast was kind enough to pass on her most ingenious method of making a kitchen range. She took a small tin of Spam, broke off the key in the usual way but left the remaining metal tag to simulate the handle on a hob lid. The tin was then opened from the underneath by means of an ordinary tin-opener, and this end became the base of the range. After a thorough wash it was painted all over with black gloss paint, and then oven doors, fire bars, hob lids and so forth were thinly outlined with grey paint. Red paint between the bars added a glow. Individual makers will be able to think up all sorts of extra embellishments, of course—curly cast iron decorations, perhaps, made from stuck-on plastic motifs, or a tile-lined alcove for the range to stand in.

Floor Coverings. If you like sewing, sumptuous floor coverings can be created in petit-point, using one strand of tapestry wool. Invent or copy a design, and draw it out on the canvas in acrylic colours first. If this is too time-consuming use velvet (which can be painted satisfactorily), short-haired fur fabric, felt, or indeed any other suitable material, avoiding coarse tweed which really does look out of scale.

Parquet blocks, wooden boards and floor tiles can be painted on paper and varnished; or, if you are not adept at painting, search for illustrations of tiles in magazines and catalogues and use those. Cork paper, tiles or table mats can be cut into little squares and stuck down to make tiled floor covering, and the flat sticks from ice cream, in sufficient quantity, will make perfect miniature floorboards. For a splendid and real-looking tile floor or surface try using little glass mosaic squares normally used for jewellery.

Once you have the basic floor covering, you can have a lot of fun making rugs. Plaited wool, wound round and round and stitched into an oval, is one idea; for a clipped rug use fine-mesh plain canvas and stitch it with large loops, cutting through them for a shaggy effect; with a darning technique, weave a rug with wool or silk, or embroider (in very fine chain stitch) a white felt numdah. Tiny scraps of material, mostly black for the best results, can be stitched to a rectangular base for a traditional rag rug. Wind thin string (dip it in coffee first for the right colour) round in flat whorls on double-sided Scotch tape stuck on a piece of card, to make a decorative 'rush' mat.

Wall Coverings. Special wallpapers for dolls' houses are obtainable from hobby shops; Miniature Mart in San Francisco has an exciting collection. Occasionally an ordinary wallpaper turns out to be suitable—one with very narrow stripes for instance—but there are many other alternatives. Artistic people can paint their own, using a small brush and water colours; the area to be covered is so small that this doesn't take too long. We've admired and tried to reproduce a striped floral pattern stencilled onto the walls of a New England bedroom in the American Museum in Britain. It seems that decorators used to travel round the American countryside undertaking this sort of work, applying their colours directly on to a white wall.

Wrapping papers with small patterns are sometimes useful, and so are pages from magazines, even if you do have to buy more than one copy to get the necessary area. Plain paper can have a cut-out frieze or panels stuck on at regular intervals. The famous Blackett Baby House in the London Museum has a dining-room decorated with a miniature version of an eighteenth-century French scenic wallpaper—just one of its many treasures. Another dolls' house we know has a genuine Randolph Caldecott nursery paper in the children's room, and many of these special wallpapers are illustrated in the growing number of books and museum publications dealing with wall coverings. Anybody looking for ideas in this field should visit Maynard Manor at John Blauer's Miniature Mart in San Francisco or the Faith Bradford dollhouse at the Smithsonian Institution in Washington, D.C. The Cooper-Hewitt Collection in New York, devoted to the history of design and the decorative arts, is another unfailing source of inspiration.

Don't forget the possibilities of fabric, which can be stuck to walls in exactly the same way as paper. It is often easier to find a printed cotton with a small floral design than a printed paper, and remnant sales are particularly good for this purpose. Other cotton prints can be found to give a *toile de Jouy* effect, and of course plain slubbed silk or a fine hessian-type material will look much the same as it would in a full-size setting.

For a luxurious look to a hall or stairway, try using thin felt. Sheets of wood veneer make realistic panelling.

Whatever material you choose, remember that doors, windows and fireplaces will take up a certain amount of space and so reduce the overall area to be covered. If you have only a very limited amount of some special wall covering then miss out the parts to be hidden by furniture and pictures.

Most ceilings look best white. Add cornices and ceiling roses of the moulded plastic intended for decorating furniture, or paint over motifs cut from thick white lace.

This seems to be the place for a heartfelt request: if you are lucky enough to be furnishing an old house, please, please, don't disturb any original decorations, however shabby they are. Any surviving scraps of wallpaper, or the printed paper floor-coverings of Victorian dolls' rooms, are of the greatest interest to collectors, and they should always be preserved *in situ* as an integral part of a period dolls' house. If you find a faded and worn appearance unsympathetic, then cover the floor harmlessly with a carpet or false floor, and the walls with an inner skin of stiff cardboard, which can be decorated in any way you choose without destroying the invaluable evidence underneath.

Windows and Curtains. A proper see-through window in the back or side wall of a miniature room might have a coloured picture or photograph of a landscape behind it—look for something appropriate on the covers of glossy magazines If possible a small gap should be left between glass and picture to give the illusion of distance, otherwise the view tends to look like a mural. One way to get the right effect is to mount the view inside a shallow cardboard box—the base of a chocolate box is ideal—and stick this box outside the window, first removing the uppermost side so that light comes in from the top. The landscape could even be changed to suit different room settings—a rural scene, a Manhattan skyline or the Golden Gate Bridge could be slotted in and out at will.

Stained glass windows made from acetate sheet painted in special transparent colours look most attractive. These colours are obtainable from hobby shops and only red, blue and yellow are needed to produce a good range of shades.

An unbroken area of glass is all right for a modern picture window, but the right sort of window panes are essential in a period room: make glazing bars from strips of balsa or matchsticks stuck neatly on to the glass, or contrive a lattice window by arranging lengths of wire in a criss-cross pattern. In both cases it helps to draw the window, exact size, on a piece of paper first, and then place the glass over this as if you were taking a tracing. Using the drawing as a guide, divide the window into separate panes by sticking on the glazing bars.

With curtains the problem is to get the material to hang correctly, rather than flying out at all angles and giving the impression that a permanent gale is blowing through the room. Use thin material, preferably already hemmed, and dampen it before pleating. Folds can also be soaked in a weak solution of cellulose wallpaper paste and then allowed to dry. Thicker curtain material can be pasted on to corrugated paper to give it natural-looking folds. Millinery velvet is by far the best if you must have velvet curtains. Narrow ribbon, braid and lampshade trimmings are useful for borders and for making valences, and fancy metal buttons make good tie-backs for formal draperies. Wooden beads will provide knobs for the ends of curtain poles, which can be made from knitting needles or lollipop sticks.

Blinds are an attractive alternative to curtains, especially in a modern house. These can be made out of paper wound round an orange stick. Venetian blinds can be made from slats of thin card threaded at each side with lengths of cotton. The technically-minded may even be able to get them to go up and down, though we've never been able to achieve this and have had to compromise by leaving them at half-mast.

In an older-type house little indoor window shutters are in keeping, made from balsa wood or thick card hinged on lengths of matching ribbon. English Victorian houses often had these shutters to keep out the cold, and so apparently did early American pioneer houses, to keep out Indian arrows.

Tiffany lamp and chandelier

Lights. The next chapter suggests ways of making various fixtures, but you could also try out a Tiffany lamp. Stick beads and a button together for the base, and use half a round ice-ball maker or half a ping-pong ball for the shade, glueing black threads across and round it to represent the squares of glass. Paint these squares with transparent paints in various colours, then stick some fine black lace round the bottom of the shade and join the shade to the base.

Make a chandelier by threading small crystal beads on fuse wire. Three hanging strings lead to one circular string, from which can be suspended loops and pendant beads.

Spotlight and wall-light

Spotlights, so often found in modern homes, can easily be made by sticking a round bead on to a short length of plastic drinking straw, and two or three of these stuck to a wooden upright, with the whole thing mounted on a wooden disc or a button, make an unusual standing lamp.

Wall lights are another feature of modern homes, and these are quickly made by sticking a bead on a loop of metal, one end of which is attached to the wall.

Wrought Iron. The string-on-Scotch-tape technique makes convincing wrought iron, but it does need careful designing. Draw out the design on card, then lay the strips of double-sided tape on top of that. Take some fairly thin string and lay that on top of the tape, following the drawn pattern. Cover the whole thing with two coats of adhesive and when dry peel off the tape and card backing. Coat with black paint and a layer of varnish. This works well for light objects, but for heavier ones the legs will have to be reinforced with wire as the stiffened string won't bear much weight.

Marbling. Marble was much used in Victorian and Regency homes and, although it is difficult to simulate with a paint brush, there is another very easy way to imitate it. Take whatever it is you wish to marble—a table top, pillar, or washstand, for example—and paint it the desired basic colour with emulsion paint. This could be pale beige, grey or white, depending on what sort of marble you have in mind. Fill a tin with cold water and drop on to its surface one or two small drips of oil paint in black or another dark colour. Swirl the water about, then quickly dip the object in and out of the water, immersing it completely. The oil colour will come off in a marble pattern. Use two colours for an even more realistic effect—black and grey on white, or dark green and beige on pale green. This technique works very well on plastic, and improves a cheap bathroom suite dramatically.

Pictures. Dolls' house walls cry out for pictures, and small illustrations from Christmas cards, magazines, catalogues and advertisements should be carefully cut out and hoarded. In a family dolls' house it might be amusing to include photographs of different generations of owner. Glaziers are usually willing to supply tiny rectangles of thin glass, or stiff transparent sheets are often used in packaging nowadays and this material is even easier to come by. Narrow strips of wood make adequate frames, but try to mitre the corners properly. A more elaborate frame can be made from the border of a stiff plastic doily: choose an oblong one rather than a round, for the sake of its straight sides, and to save time look out for one that is already coloured gold. Brass curtain rings are just the right frames for miniature portraits and silhouettes.

A stately home for dolls could include a picture gallery hung with tightly-packed Old Masters, with perhaps a classical statue or two from a Greek tourist shop. Only the minimum of furniture would be needed—say a console table and an upholstered seat.

Toys. Be sure to include a nursery if you are designing a dolls' house for a large family. Some miniature playthings can go in just as they are—very small teddy bears, tiny dolls, a minute abacus and a rubber ball; there is also a nice little blackboard and easel amongst the commercially made dolls' house accessories. A matchbox standing on its side and stuck to a base becomes the foundation of a miniature dolls' house. A Noah's Ark is not too difficult if you choose the simpler variety on a flat, raft-like base. There are many beautifully illustrated books on period toys, and if you can get hold of one of these you will find it gives you more ideas. For instance a strip of square-section wood could be carefully cut into cubes to form old-fashioned building bricks decorated with letters of the alphabet; a paper kite with a bright tail is another possibility. The scrap screen described previously is particularly suitable for a Victorian nursery, and animals from plastic farmyard sets can be adapted to make rocking horses and pull-along toys. Solve the problem of wheels by using buttons or nameless oddments from the bottom of the tool box; defunct electrical fittings always seem to be a mine of bright metal washers with a hundred and one uses for the model-maker.

Ornaments. So many things come into this category that it's impossible to list more than a few. But take clocks, for example: lovely decorative clocks can be made from the face of a toy wrist watch surrounded by an ornate setting of modelling material. Note, too, the excellent grandfather clocks amongst the commercially-made dolls' house furniture.

China ornaments are easily moulded—those familiar Staffordshire dogs are a simple shape to copy and look like the real thing when painted and varnished. A fish tank, or a wall case for a stuffed pike, can be constructed from small oblongs of acetate glued together at the corners, although at the moment an excellent dolls' house aquarium is available from toyshops.

66

Staffordshire dogs and a simple shape to copy

Flat buttons can be painted with small flowers to look like rare china, as can halves of ice cube balls, though you have to stand them on a button to make them steady. Ornaments under glass domes look particularly well in period dolls' houses, and to imitate these use acetate fishing floats cut in half. Arrange small shells underneath, or even budgerigar feathers clipped to look like Victorian feather flowers. A 'wax' doll, a wedding-cake bird or some tiny flowers from the millinery department are also suitable for displaying under glass, and anyone who is especially good at these miniature arrangements will find it worth while to invest in the real glass domes, with proper bases, which are made for confirmed dolls' house addicts. Accessories of this sort—and new ones are constantly coming on to the market —are advertised in a monthly magazine called *Doll House (and Miniature) News*. No serious collector can afford to be without this admirable little publication, which is available by subscription from:

> Doll House (and Miniature) News
> Marian O'Brien, Editor
> 3 Orchard Lane
> Kirkwood, Missouri 63122

At present an annual subscription costs $5.00.

A miniature room hung with paper-chains, holly and so

forth would make a pretty Christmas decoration. A Christmas tree could be added (most stores stock little conical trees in red tubs) and this could have glass beads for baubles. Sprigs of holly can usually be found with the cake decorations. Tiny parcels could be wrapped in gold and silver foil and coloured tissue paper, and a dining table with a snowy cloth could be draped with swags of absorbant cotton. With oil paints and modelling compound, a rich dark Christmas pudding would be the work of a moment, and a wintry scene outside the window would give the final seasonal touch.

Found Objects

THERE ARE all kinds of short cuts to be taken when filling a dolls' house. The art lies in recognising small things which at first sight appear to have nothing to do with miniature furnishings, but which with a few minor adjustments—or indeed often just as they are—can be used alongside custom-built dolls' house accessories. In real life a decorator would probably call such windfalls *objets trouvés*, but the less grandiose popular version, found objects, seems a more appropriate description for the modest bits and pieces which have found their way into our various dolls' houses.

Their great advantage is that they save such an enormous amount of time. A small cardboard box, for instance, can be the right size for a cupboard or the base of a bed; two or three matchboxes put together may prove to be the right size for a fireplace, an ornate brooch will save having to make a picture frame, or you may come across an odd bit of plastic that will form part of a table or a chair. The tops of bottles, jars and tubes provide several useful shapes: a toothpaste cap makes an excellent flower pot if turned upside down, filled with sand and planted with a twig or artificial flower. Other tubes, like those for shaving cream, have larger tops which can be treated in the same way, and a row of assorted colours and sizes standing on a shelf or window sill is very effective. Small caps, especially white ones, are also ideal for beakers. The raw materials you need are all about you, so don't throw any odds and ends away but store them in a large box or bag until you

69

Toothpaste caps make miniature flower pots

need them. Then all you have to do is look at them with a fresh eye and translate them into their new existence.

There are some examples of furnishings which need no adaptation at all, and which can go straight into a dolls' house just as they are.

Pill jars as storage containers

Chemists often put pills into tiny glass jars, which should be kept to build up a row of storage containers, and filled with hundreds-and-thousands, flour, ground coffee and sago. Labels should be added (perhaps cut out of a coloured magazine illustration) and buttons for lids. If the pill bottles are made of plastic, as many are now, the thread part of the neck can be sawn off, leaving a better-proportioned storage jar.

Metal crown corks with a crinkly edge, upside down, make decorative bowls for fruit or flowers.

70

Ornaments come from broken jewellery, especially rings and charm bracelets; from Christmas crackers, perfume bottle tops, and decorated thimbles (for a really pretty vase, turn a painted china thimble upside down with its convex tip resting in the hollow of a suitable button). Small plastic creatures like rabbits and chickens from a child's farmyard set are good ornaments for the chimney-piece.

One of the most popular Victorian seaside souvenirs was a minute pair of ivory binoculars, with a magnifying glass at one end and a photograph of a local view let in at the other; an astonishing number of these ingenious trifles

Toy sentry for a dolls' house nursery

have survived, and one often sees them in old dolls' houses. Although there is nothing quite so nice in today's souvenir shops, they do sometimes have very small brass candlesticks, chandeliers, copper saucepans, cauldrons, buckets, colanders, filigree metal tables, rocking chairs with pincushions let into the seats, grandfather clocks and ceramic fireplaces. Don't be put off by the civic coat of arms, the egg-timers or the good luck symbols which are usually attached to these miniatures, as they can almost always be prised off or obliterated without any difficulty. Whole

71

armies of plastic knights in full armour are lined up in souvenir shops at the moment, very cheap and extremely useful for giving a baronial touch to a dolls' house hall. Overseas tourist haunts have exotic variations on the same theme: if you have friends going to Mexico, for example, ask them to look out for little wooden shelves loaded with rustic earthenware pots and pans. Limoges porcelain from France is exquisite and much more expensive, but a painted plate hanging in a drawing-room, or a candlestick beside a draped tester bed, will lift any dolls' house into the luxury class.

Some ironmongers sell brass or ormolu mounts which translate well into dolls' house terms: classical vase-shaped finials simply become classical vases; swags, bows and beading are all invaluable for white-and-gold drawing-rooms, and merry little cherubs intended for decorating clock faces are equally suitable for dolls' house overmantels or for holding the drapery above a miniature bed.

Key-rings are another source of supply. We have found

Plastic knight in armour

rings with all sorts of miniature attachments, including a football, football boots, skating boots with steel skates, boxing gloves, a metal tankard and, best of all, a terrestrial globe which really turns round on its stand.

Key-ring globe and wedding cake pillar

Cake decorations are useful too. Wedding-cake pillars make elegant pedestals for halls and drawing-rooms, white plaster birds can be transformed into ornaments or used in decorative schemes, and candle holders for birthday cakes provide nursery playthings—trains, toy soldiers and animals. The same sort of shops usually sell packets of plastic cocktail sticks with fancy ends: some are miniature wine-glasses which, sawn off from the stick part, make colourful Venetian goblets for dolls.

We envy Victorian collectors the lovely little pictures called Baxter prints taken off needle packets and hung on dolls' house walls, but in due course today's pictorial postage stamps will probably be just as sought-after. A strip cut from a gold-embossed paper cake-frill makes an excellent frame for these 'oil paintings'.

Now for a few objects which need a little adaptation before being put to their new use. The only time-consuming part is waiting for the paint to dry when things have to be coloured, but this can be cut down by using quick-drying emulsion or lacquer paint.

Kitchen Ware

The very small moulds intended for chocolates or *petits fours* make full-size baking tins for dolls' house kitchens. They come in assorted shapes—round, oval and diamond—with fluted sides, and look very decorative. Some are like jelly-moulds, and these can be painted over with copper paint and hung on the wall.

Copper saucepan. Small pans are difficult to make, but a giant-sized pan (it would measure 16 inches diameter in real life) can be made from a plastic baby-food measure with its handle trimmed. It was also painted in copper paint, and a large button with a black bead on it formed the lid.

Sugar canister. The clear plastic top of a tube, turned upside down, forms a canister, which is then fitted with a button lid.

Dish. The edges of a plastic bottle cap cut in a fluted shape, then painted white with a pattern added becomes a dish.

Trays. Tin lids make good 'cheap tin trays', particularly the round press-on ones with a raised rim which gives an authentic-looking finish. Tin can be painted to resemble Pontypool or Russian ware, or just decorated with a small picture cut out of a magazine, varnished.

Plates. Buttons come in many different styles, and flattish ones will do for plates, with the holes either filled in or covered with a stick-on design.

74

Living Rooms
Look out for fancy buttons to turn into wall plaques; a plain black button, upside down, is often just the right ebony-type stand for a tiny ornament which looks insignificant without a base.

Glass lamp base and shade. Small perfume bottles are very useful things to keep. We turned one into an attractive lamp by fitting it with a fluted shade made of a circle of paper upon which are stuck lengths of pale blue plastic drinking straws. The shade is attached to the base by a cardboard collar.

Oil lamp   *Chandelier*

Oil lamp. An old-fashioned oil lamp can be made from a couple of brass necklace fittings stuck on to a fancy bead. This forms the base, on to which is stuck another brass fitting and a spherical white bead to represent the glass globe.

Chandelier. A strange plastic fitting with twelve small sockets in it inspired an elegant chandelier. It's joined to a plastic bottle top, which forms the base of the chandelier, and painted gold. Lengths of white plastic drinking straws are stuck into each socket to represent candles. The chandelier is suspended by a central wire.

75

 *Decanter*

Decanter. Another use for a small perfume bottle is as a decanter. Discard the plastic top and substitute a suitable glass bead stopper.

Two hanging mirrors and a jewelled book

Frames. The decorative top and bottom of an ornamental mirror were two necklace clasps. These were stuck on to a piece of gold-painted plastic, on to which was stuck a small piece of mirror paper. Another looking-glass was made from a handbag mirror with an old metal buckle, minus its centre bar, stuck on to make a sumptuous frame. Yet another frame, this time for an Old Master picture cut out of a print catalogue, started life as a junk-jewellery brooch. A modern frame was made from the plastic lid of a small butter container.

Jewelled book. This was a necklace clasp that just happened to look exactly like one of those bound and jewelled volumes you sometimes see in historic houses and museums —an added touch of splendour for any dolls' house.

Television set

Television set. This was very easy to make, out of a white plastic razor-blade dispenser. We tucked a magazine picture inside the 'screen' (which used to contain the razor

Hat rack and stag's head

blades) and covered it with acetate. Three little·black beads form the control knobs and four lengths of plastic straw the legs. Another television set came ready-made out of a Christmas cracker.

Hat rack. We found a brass fitting that must once have been part of a door lock. Painted white, given three little plastic knobs (map pins inside white plastic straws) and a piece of mirror, it makes an unusual, rather Victorian-looking, hatstand.

Mounted stag's head. Another period piece for the hall, easily contrived by beheading a cheap plastic toy stag (or perhaps a buffalo) and gluing the sawn-off neck to a shield-shaped piece of stained (try dark brown boot-polish) wood. Really dedicated miniaturists then start worrying about how to make use of the left-over legs!

77

Bath

Upstairs

Old fashioned bath. We came by a transparent plastic jam dish on an Italian holiday and, knowing it would come in useful one day, brought it home. It's just the shape for a miniature bath. Painted with white emulsion paint and stood on four collar-stud legs, it has silver paper taps and a plug hole made from a small gold bracelet link. A floral pattern drawn on the inside of the bath in felt-nib pen adds the finishing touch.

Bathroom light. A flat white glass bead in a silver mounting once formed the clasp for a necklace; with hooks and additions removed, it makes a fine bathroom light.

Outside

Flower trough. The plastic flip top of a package stands on balsa wood feet and is filled with plastic cement earth, into which is stuck a variety of dried or artificial flowers.

Garden table

Wrought iron garden table. A large pierced button, mounted on a plastic tube top, makes a convincing white 'wrought iron' garden table.

Tenants for a Dolls' House

THERE ARE definitely two schools of thought about dolls for dolls' houses. Some collectors prefer to display miniature furniture on its own, and feel that stiff little dolls are a distraction; others think a dolls' house looks awfully unpopulated without tenants—rather like that ill-fated brig, the *Marie Celeste* which, you may recall, was found in mid-ocean, all sails set, meal untouched on the table, and no sign of the crew.

On the whole, model rooms furnished with exquisite replicas tend to be doll-less, while dolls' houses meant to be playthings have inhabitants. Thus Queen Mary's Dolls' House at Windsor Castle and Mrs Carlisle's famous miniature rooms (now on view to the public at Grey's Court, Henley-on-Thames) rely on the perfection of their scaled-down furnishings, while Ann Sharp's Baby House at Norwich is unimaginable without its beady-eyed, waxen occupants. Of all tiny dolls, Ann Sharp's are the most evocative, for they are still labelled with the names she pinned on them almost 300 years ago: 'my lord Rochett', 'Mrs. Hannah, ye housekeeper' and 'Sarah Gill, child's maid' are just three members of the household. Today's children still get the same pleasure out of a family of dolls for their houses, which they can move from room to room and invent stories for. So far as adult collectors are

79

concerned it is really a matter of personal choice, and you either like dolls or you don't. If you don't, then you can safely skip the rest of this chapter.

As with the furniture, it helps to get dolls' house dolls into historical perspective. The earliest ones seem usually to have been made of wax, which was used to model pale ladies dressed in brocade and gentlemen in powdered wigs, robust servants toiling in the kitchen and fragile babies— sometimes twins, as at Uppark—lying in wicker cradles. Tiny wooden dolls were far stronger, and early ones—dating from say the beginning of the nineteenth century—can often be identified by the yellow combs in their black painted coiffures. Similar little figures were produced until well into the twentieth century, and a few, said to be the remains of a hoard discovered in a barn in the Dolomites quite recently, are currently on sale in certain specialist toyshops. Small dolls with a china head and limbs attached to a sawdust-filled cotton torso were made in many different styles from about the middle of the nineteenth century until the outbreak of World War II: the mid-Victorian version has come to be regarded as the typical dolls' house doll, with shiny black hair, pink cheeks and tiny feet encased in moulded boots. Besides these there were others made from the finest parian, with beautifully detailed hairstyles, and later, cheaper, ones with a matt, rather coarse, finish.

Miniature dolls with jointed all-china bodies, inset glass eyes and real hair wigs seem to date from about 1900, and they are very attractive indeed, especially if their original clothes have survived. In the 1920s and 1930s there were fragile celluloid dolls, German or Japanese, horribly susceptible to both fire and accidental crushing; despite these hazards, though, many have been preserved.

All these dolls, even the celluloid ones, have now become collector's items and to the uninitiated they sound very, very expensive. They *can* still be found—after all, they were turned out by the million—but the only sources of supply we know are specialist dealers, and prices are uniformly high. Whether one invests or not depends upon personal inclination and circumstances, but perhaps it's worth bearing in mind that a good little Victorian doll, in original clothes, would probably cost less than a fairly modest dinner for two in a restaurant. Occasionally one hears the most tantalising stories of lucky buys at country auctions, or surprising results from a newspaper advertisement, but by and large the fact remains that period dolls' house dolls are not in the bargain class.

One solution is to recreate them as nearly as possible, though with the idea of producing acceptable substitutes rather than fakes. Old-fashioned wooden clothes pegs can be turned into delightful little dolls, full-length for men and women, half-length for children, just by drawing on a face and adding pipe-cleaner arms. Everything depends on how skillfully they are dressed, and here again it pays to take great care with fabrics and use only non-synthetics and mellow colours when aiming for a 'period' look.

In the United States there are kits on sale which include china heads and limbs for making up into Victorian-style dolls. Although they aren't cheap they are beautifully made, and the results are excellent. However, anyone with patience and a flair for modelling can reproduce something very similar, and it is a great help to be able to borrow a genuine, preferably undressed, dolls' house doll to measure and copy. Most collectors are generous people, and a lot of lending, exchanging and information-swapping goes on in doll clubs. A careful examination will show how the head-and-shoulders piece is glued to the cloth body, and how the lower arms and legs are joined to narrow fabric tubes, which allow a certain amount of movement—the diagram is probably easier to grasp than written instructions. There are various modelling compounds on the market, and most of those intended for amateurs do not need firing in a kiln—they just harden as they dry out. One hesitates to mention particular brands because

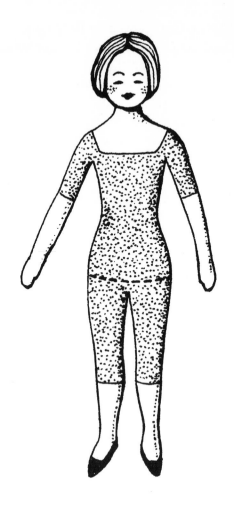

Traditional dolls' house doll

manufacturers have a tendency to cease production without warning, or distribution is limited to certain parts of the country. Anyone with access to a kiln can use clay and have their models fired, but remember there will be shrinkage in either case. Don't attempt anything too detailed in the way of features on this scale, or your dolls will end up looking like Cyrano de Bergerac—an egg shape for the head and two indentations for eye sockets is really enough.

Hair and features should be painted on, and then the whole head-and-shoulders given a coat of clear varnish. Instead of a painted hairstyle, a wig can be cut from a hank of fine dolls' hair obtainable from some haberdashery counters, and this can be curled round a hot skewer or nail. Boots or shoes should be moulded in one piece with the legs, and painted; flat boots are earlier, for dolls, than boots with little heels.

If this sounds too time-consuming and complicated, remember that clothes cover a multitude of sins and omissions. Forearms *can* be matchsticks, slightly shaped and then sandpapered. Legs can be omitted altogether if the doll is to wear a long skirt—a paper or buckram petticoat will enable it to stand up.

Period costume is a subject on its own, of course, and if you want to pin your dolls' house down to a particular time you will have to make sure the dolls' clothes match the furniture and general décor. One of the most celebrated dolls' house experts, Miss Faith Eaton, has produced a wonderful set of patterns for tiny clothes covering each decade of the nineteenth century, together with details of the sort of dolls which would have worn them. Master and mistress, children and servants are all included and any reader will be lost in admiration for the painstaking research which has gone into Miss Eaton's delightful book.*
Non-traditional dolls for modern houses can be made in various ways, and they don't have to be either elaborate or costly. The main requirements are that they should be the right size for the rooms so that they don't tower over the furniture in a sinister manner, and that they should be able

* To be published by G. Bell and Sons Ltd., London, England.

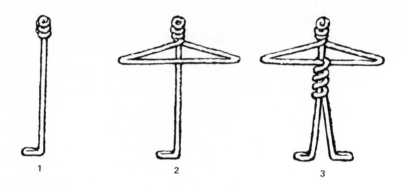

Three pipe cleaners twisted into basic doll shape

to bend or move their legs in order to sit down. The most striking thing about old dolls is the way they loll about on sofas in a decidedly inebriated way.

One of the easiest types to tackle is made from pipe cleaners and a wooden bead. If you can't find a suitable bead, mould a head or simply use padding. Three pipe-cleaners should be twisted as shown in the diagram. Pad the body and the tops of the legs, head (if necessary) and feet with Kleenex tissues, then bind the whole doll with flesh-coloured wool. Wind the wool firmly round the body, head (if padded) and limbs, sticking with a dab of adhesive as you go round the corners so that the wool doesn't slip off the ends of the feet or the dome of the head. You can either draw a face with felt-nib pen, paint it, or embroider the padded variety with cottons.

The hair is lengths of wool stuck on with fabric adhesive —the girl has longer hair than the boy and we frayed the wool to make it look wavy. The girl wears a long tube-shaped dress gathered at the neck and trimmed with lace, topped by a pink felt waistcoat and a paper hat trimmed with dried flowers. Her feet were dipped into white plastic cement to make trendy boots. A boy can be dressed in jacket and trousers. His outfit is completed by a ribbon scarf, with a hand-drawn design on it, a chain belt, and plastic wood boots which enable him to stand firmly.

84

Finished pipe cleaner doll

This basic construction method is capable of endless variations, depending on the materials to hand. Wire can replace pipe cleaners, narrow strips of soft rag can replace Kleenex tissues and wool. Any knitted fabric—non-sheer stockings for example—can be sewn into little tubes to cover arms and legs, where stretchiness is most useful. Sealing wax will do for feet.

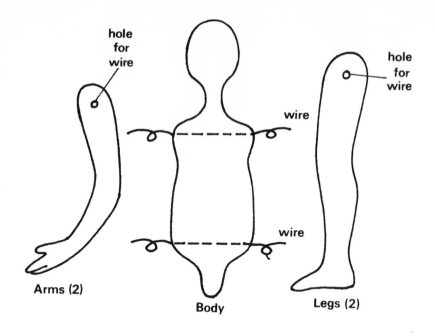

hole for wire

Arms (2)

hole for wire

wire

wire

Body

Legs (2)

Shapes for moulded doll

We have already looked at the possibilities of using modelling compounds to reproduce small Victorian dolls, but the same sort of process can be used for easy-to-make modern dolls too. In this case the material used, bought in a craft shop, had to be baked in a domestic oven to harden it, but full instructions were given on the packet. To make the moulded doll, first mould the shapes shown in the drawing, making sure the base of the torso is flat enough for the doll to be able to sit down comfortably. Insert the wire before heating the modelling compound, and after the shapes have been hardened in the oven thread the wires from the torso through the holes in the tops of the arms and legs. Paint the body and face flesh colour, and protect the paint with a layer of varnish.

Our doll has hair made of hanks cut from a piece of long-haired fur fabric, stuck to the skull and arranged in a

Doll made of modelling compound

becoming way, then secured with 'hairpins' made of sawn-off brass pins. She wears a grey felt skirt and a white, long-sleeved blouse trimmed with lace at the neck and down the front. The sleeves are made separately, then stuck into the armholes.

A child doll can easily be made by the same method, but it's important to remember that children aren't miniature adults—they have much larger heads in relation to their bodies.

87

String doll

Another easy doll can be made from string. For this type, take two pieces of coarse twine or string about 5 inches long and thread one end of each of them through a large oval pink bead so that 1 inch of string sticks out of the top. Fray these ends and stick them down over the bead to form hair. A third piece of string forms the arms, which are bound to the doll's trunk with strips of non-woven fabric. This material also serves as a padding, and the ends are stuck down with fabric adhesive. The two long ends of string form legs and feet, and are bound with fabric in the same way as the trunk. Then the face is painted, and the doll dressed.

There is quite an assortment of small plastic dolls in the shops nowadays, and these can be very useful, especially if one wants extra-fast results. They are much improved by having their rough pink plastic edges filed off, and by new hair of fur fabric, wool, silk or proper doll's wigging; it even makes a great difference just to paint their pink pates a good dark brown.

Careful dressing transforms these ordinary little dolls, and it's important to get the basic shape of the clothes right. If in doubt as to whether or not a garment will wrap itself comfortably round a doll, cut out a pattern first in a spare piece of material and drape it until it hangs as it should, and then use it as the basis for the finished garment. Non-woven lining material is ideal for small clothes because it doesn't fray and is firm enough to have small patterns painted on it; felt has the same advantages. If you use ordinary material, try not to leave raw edges but turn them under and stick them with a smear of fabric adhesive, applied with an orange stick. When dressing such small dolls aim for a general effect rather than bothering with details like buttons and poppers—in fact we would never advise trying to make clothes which can be taken off, as it just isn't worth the effort. The best way to get garments to fit smoothly is to sew them on firmly, keeping underclothing to a minimum.

Knitted and crocheted clothes turn out surprisingly well, and lengths of ribbon and lace are invaluable. Pieces cut from worn-out socks and jerseys are useful too, because wool stretches and moulds itself so satisfactorily.

Shoes are difficult to manage on a small scale, and it's perhaps wiser to give the dolls boots made from plastic

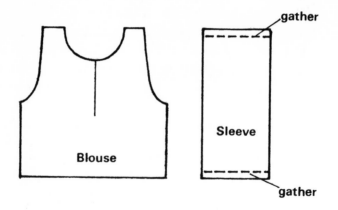

Blouse pattern. Cut back and front the same. Slit down front only

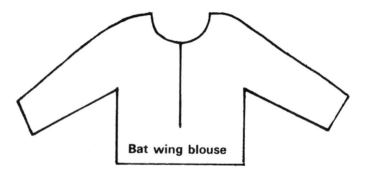

wood or cement, or paint on shoes and stockings.

All trimmings and accessories (handbags, belts, jewellery) must be small. A length of disused pendant chain makes a good chain belt or handbag handle. An old kid glove will provide enough soft leather for innumerable belts, hand-bags, and waistcoats. Tiny beads simulate buttons. A cylinder of fur fabric becomes a muff for a doll in outdoor clothes, and a cloak or cape is quicker to make than a coat.

An old handkerchief can be turned into a pretty summer dress for a doll; take advantage of the narrow hem and the design round the border. Woolworths sell cheap handker-chiefs printed with tiny flowers which are ideal.

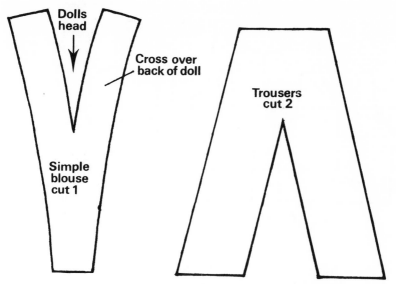

Dolls head

Cross over back of doll

Trousers cut 2

Simple blouse cut 1

Blouse. Take under doll between legs and stick to back crossover piece. Trousers. Stick down side seams

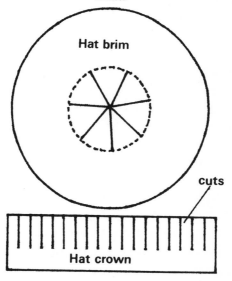

Hat brim

cuts

Hat crown

Cut and bend up segments on hat brim. Bend crown of hat into a circle and overlap and stick cuts over your finger to make crown. Stick round brim segments

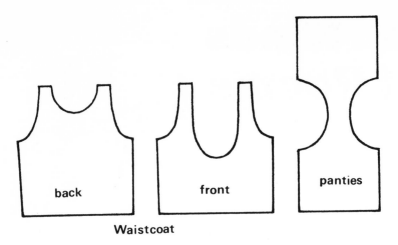

Waistcoat

Waistcoat and panties. Stick seams

One final thought: dolls' house women have always heavily outnumbered dolls' house men. There was even a *Punch* joke about this discrepancy in 1872 and a miniature Victorian paterfamilias is worth about three times as much as his female relations.

Animals
No home is complete without a dog or cat. Cage birds are also popular in dolls' houses, and Mrs. Graham Greene has even found a dolls' kitchen where 'a hedgehog patrols to keep down the black-beetles'.

Small bisque animals from the nineteenth and early twentieth century are relatively plentiful, and there is a good selection of modern china cats and dogs in gift shops.

Dogs and cats can be made at home from pipe cleaners: make the skeleton first, and then wind more pipe cleaners round and round for a fluffy look. The animals can be left white, or spotted or coloured with ink or water colour. An alternative technique is to pad the skeleton with Kleenex tissue moulded to shape with fabric adhesive; this compound can be painted, sandpapered and varnished.

All Kinds of Rooms

Furnishing Four Individual Rooms

To ILLUSTRATE what we have been talking about so far, four rooms were furnished from scratch. The first (page 101) was the drawing-room of an 1860s dolls' house—a beautiful toy with a fine classical facade complete with balcony and imposing portico. This is the sort of house so often found in museum collections, with its original wallpapers intact, every piece of furniture miraculously preserved and rosy-cheeked china dolls still *in situ*. A little careful research and a few visits to specialised collections soon shows the effect to aim for: a multitude of gilt-framed pictures, mahogany furniture, bird-cages, over-stuffed upholstery and a general abundance of *bric-à-brac*. As always with dolls' houses, the mid-Victorian model reflects contemporary design and the contemporary middle-class way of life, and for this most lavish of periods there is no shortage of ideas about what to put in—the difficulty lies in deciding what gems must be left out.

In an old house of this calibre the purist would allow only equally old furniture, taking infinite pains to track down the ravishing little rosewood sewing tables, embroidery frames, purple velvet sofas and glass-domed clocks which formed the ordinary stock-in-trade of any Dickensian toyshop. There are dedicated collectors on both sides of the Atlantic who will cheerfully spend a small fortune with the dealers who specialise in old dolls and dolls' houses, who will get up at dawn to be first in the field at street markets,

93

and who haunt the more fashionable salerooms (rather pointless, this, in our experience, since the dealers are always there too). Their dolls are invariably dressed in old fabrics of exactly the right vintage, and some are even rumoured to sew with genuinely old thread. But the more restrained enthusiast will probably be content to compromise—a few original old pieces, eked out with careful copies.

For our drawing-room we were lucky enough to start off with an authentic Victorian sewing table, tallboy and glass-fronted display cabinet, with an ormolu clock and a terrestrial globe for ornaments. The house itself set the period—the mid-1860s—so that nothing going into the room could be later than this. However obvious this may sound, in practice anachronisms can slip into a dolls' house all too easily: after all, without recourse to an encyclopaedia it's difficult to be dogmatic about exactly when musical boxes gave way to wind-up gramophones with green trumpets, or daffodil-shaped telephones to the type of model in use today.

But to start at the beginning: the room was 15 inches wide by 13 inches deep, and like all old dolls' house rooms it was disproportionately tall, with a ceiling height of over 12 inches. A convenient scale to settle on was therefore 1 inch to 1 foot. The ceiling was painted white, and for lack of any Victorian-looking paper the walls were painted apple-green. Wall decoration for a period house is always a problem, so few old papers having survived. One expert makes wonderful use of decorative end-papers from Victorian books, which is all right provided the books are dull enough to warrant their being dismembered, and there are enough of them to yield the necessary area of wall-covering. To give interest to our walls we stuck on plastic swags sold by the strip in most home-decorating shops; this will upset the purists, but when painted white these swags really do look like plaster, and their classical design strikes the right note in a fairly formal room of this character.

The floor was covered with dark green velvet, but for anyone with time to spare a needlework carpet, based on a nineteenth-century floral pattern, would be a delightful thing to make. The motifs would have to be simplified, of course, since not even the most fervent needlewoman would want to reproduce *gros-point* to a 1:12 scale. But many Victorian mothers and loving aunts managed to work out most effective designs for dolls' carpets and rugs, stitching away by the light of oil lamps with left-overs from their gaudy Berlin woolwork.

The cherished pieces of 'Duncan Phyfe' furniture went in next, with the sewing table prominently displayed near the front. The tallboy and the cabinet fitted into the alcoves on either side of the fireplace.

The first thing to make was a sofa—a typical mid-nineteenth-century dolls' house toy which anyone who has looked at a few old houses will easily recognise. It was made of thin wood and upholstered in faded old damask, following the sofa instructions on pages 32–33. Much the same construction method was used for the small sewing chair,

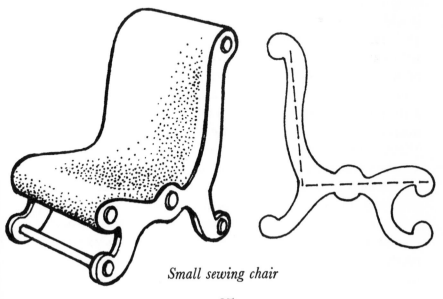

Small sewing chair

95

except that as an experiment this was copied from a real piece of furniture and not an old toy. On the whole, though, when recreating a dolls' room of this sort it is more realistic-looking, and certainly easier, to copy old pieces of toy furniture rather than scale down human-size Victoriana, and try to reproduce that.

The curvy spoon-back chair was made of plastic wood built up on a framework of pipe cleaners, with green silk upholstery caught down with minute stitches to imitate buttoning. The footstool was the end cut off a wooden cotton reel, stained and highly polished, with a padded *petit-point* top and four bead feet. By the way, wooden cotton reels should be carefully hoarded, as the new spools are plastic; a good thing for the world's tree population, no doubt, but a sad loss for amateur toy-makers who for generations have relied on empty spools not only for miniature furniture but also for wheels, flower pots, windmills and lighthouses.

The round table in the middle of the room was a modern one from a cheap mass-produced set, but it was used because the size and shape were suitable, and it meant yet another surface to load with ornaments. An easy alternative would have been a circle of thick cardboard glued on top of a couple of cotton reels, the whole structure hidden under a floor-sweeping cloth: a good way to disguise a makeshift table of any dimension, whether for dolls or people.

Going back to found objects, a wedding-cake pillar made a marble stand for a small metal ewer—the dolls' house equivalent of the Portland Vase—but a tiny parian statue or a bust of some sober statesman would have been just as suitable. (Devotees of *The Wind in the Willows* will remember Mole's modest little home with its 'brackets carrying plaster statuary—Garibaldi, and the infant Samuel, and Queen Victoria, and other heroes of modern Italy'. Surely Kenneth Grahame must have first seen these charming oddments in a dolls' house?) A plain oblong wooden snuff-box, black with a few lines of inlay on the lid, made a con-

96

vincing musical box just as it was. The oil lamp, on the other hand, needed quite a lot of contrivance, as it was assembled from an elaborate glass bead mounted on a button (the base), a twist of fuse wire (the metal fitting), a frosted plastic ball (the globe) and a short length of glass tubing from a broken light bulb (the chimney).
from a broken light bulb (the chimney).

The great thing to aim for in a room of this period is the widest possible assortment of mid-Victorian clutter which, however undesirable in real life, is unfailingly endearing when reduced to dolls' house size. To help with the overall impression we hung heavy silk window curtains from a mahogany rail (an old wooden knitting needle stained dark brown, with jump links for rings), with figured white lace curtains too, to reinforce the shut-in feeling. The sofa was heaped with cushions, and all available surfaces piled with ornaments, albums, work-boxes, knitting and half-finished embroidery; these objects were added from time to time, as they happened to turn up, or as one of us was inspired to make them.

The pictures were especially important, with such high walls to fill. The best frames for an old house like this are those little gilt ones which originally came with daguerreo-types, all enclosed in a velvet-lined case. There used to be plenty on junk stalls, still complete with portraits of be-shawled grannies or serious small girls. Like everything else they are scarcer now and more expensive, and even the photographs have acquired a period charm so that one hesitates to wash poor granny off and re-use the clear glass. But if you can bear to, these frames do set off dolls' house pictures beautifully. We used colour reproductions of con-temporary works (taking care to check that the originals were already in existence in the 1860s) and some earlier silhouettes, cut from museum postcards and framed in brass curtain rings. When you can find them Baxter prints, with their incredible detail, make superb miniature master-pieces; Landseer is another Victorian artist whose works seem to have a special affinity with the dolls' house world.

As this room was very much a toy it had to have dolls. An original china-headed family of the period would have been ideal, with a moustachio'd father and a selection of demure ladies with elaborate hairstyles and flat-heeled black boots; but as dolls like this are rarities now and very expensive even when they can be found, the room was peopled instead with newly-bought 'peg woodens', carefully dressed in 1860s costume. These are direct descendants of the traditional 'Dutch' dolls mentioned by Dickens in *The Cricket on the Hearth*: digressing on levels of dolls' house society, he contrasts them with aristocratic wax dolls and calls them 'the common people' with 'just so many matches out of the tinder-boxes for their arms and legs'. With such good authority to rely on, we felt quite justified in using wooden dolls in this mid-Victorian setting, even though we were up-grading them socially by establishing them in a drawing-room which fairly breathed middle-class lavishness, ostentation, leisure, warmth and comfort.

The second room (see page 102) was the re-creation of a small bedroom furnished in the early 1900s when the pendulum had swung away from all the over-elaboration and gaudy colours of the mid-nineteenth century. The setting was a three-sided box, rather like a stage set, made from some lengths of wood discarded by a carpenter: it cost nothing apart from the price of a tube of glue and a few small, fine nails which had to be bought specially. A dolls' room of this type has a long history, for some of the very earliest, the so-called Nuremberg kitchens, were built on the same plan. It is equally good for rooms, shops or copies of that most enchanting of French toys, a model schoolroom complete with desks, blackboard, slates, books, globes and dark-pinafored children. It has the advantage, too, of taking up very little space.

Our model was $11\frac{1}{2}$ inches wide, $9\frac{1}{2}$ inches deep from back to front, and 9 inches high; there was no need for the

98

walls to be any higher as there was to be no ceiling and hence no difficulty about having to peer into a small enclosed space. The four pieces of wood were simply cut out with an ordinary saw, sand-papered vigorously and then fixed together with glue and small nails tapped in through carefully drilled holes. Anything in the way of dovetailing or any special carpentry skill is quite unnecessary—all one has to be able to do is measure accurately.

The idea for a William Morris/art nouveau room came with the discovery that the Victoria and Albert Museum, at South Kensington, sold coloured postcards of an 1892 wallpaper called 'Blackthorn' which was designed by Morris himself. A surprising number of cards, eighteen in fact, was needed to cover the three walls, but with the pattern painstakingly matched the final result was well worth the expense—the model (page 103) looks like a William Morris room viewed through the wrong end of a telescope.

The floor was left bare, with lines scored into the wood to represent boards. Slight variations between one board and another were brushed on with water-colours, and then the whole floor was varnished. The skirting was a strip of natural wood.

There is a special type of fumed oak dolls' house furniture with an art nouveau look about it, which one soon comes to recognise after looking at a few collections. It is absolutely unmistakable, with a peculiar period flavour quite distinct from the earlier, glossy pieces. A sturdy cupboard of this sort gave the bedroom a flying start and, with the authentic wallpaper, set the style for the rest of the furniture, which was nearly all home-made.

This was the time when Morris's designs, and those of his disciples, were having a profound influence on furnishing and decoration. Besides the challenge of creating an unusual dolls' house, a study of the decorative schemes, the manufacturing techniques and the crafts revival of the period is a fascinating exercise, leading the researcher along innumerable tangents in the way of biographies, pattern

99

books, catalogues (in particular the 1970 reissue of the 1907 Army and Navy Stores catalogue), old photographs and out-of-the-way museums; it was only when we began planning this room that we finally managed to get out to Walthamstow, in east London, to visit the William Morris Gallery there. A collection like this provides enough ideas to furnish ten rooms—muted colours everywhere, sage greens, soft blues, pinks and warm browns; Celtic motifs, floral rugs, simple brass candlesticks and wall sconces, medieval-looking portraits, bronzes, arts-and-crafts firescreens, stained glass, painted tiles, embroideries and rush-seated chairs.

Coming back to our miniature room, we decided on a simple wooden bed, with rails at the top and bottom. We added a plain white coverlet, though an embroidered bedcover, inspired by the one May Morris made for her father, is on the agenda for next winter. Although bathrooms were gradually coming into general use, a bedroom of this time would almost certainly still have had a ewer and basin on a washstand: the washstand was made from natural wood, in an easy-to-copy straight-sided shape, with a row of William de Morgan tiles (cut from a magazine picture) along the back. The ewer, basin and the pot under the bed were lucky finds in an antique market. Toy pottery like this was made for dolls' houses until the 1930s, and is not all that difficult to come by even today.

The rush-seated chair was typically 'Morris and Company' and was in fact copied from an illustration in one of the firm's catalogues. The basic framework was fine dowelling (lollipop and cocktail sticks do very well), with the rails at the back of the chair cut from slivers of thin wood, steamed and then dried into the required very slight curve. The seat was filled in just as those of real chairs would be, except that fine strands of raffia were used instead of rushes.

We found a little blonde doll of the right period for the room, and dressed her in a Liberty print. Books were provided (French poetry seemed suitable) and a wind-up

Victorian drawing-room

(Drawing by Roger Banks-Pye)

An ornate bedroom

(Drawing by Roger Banks-Pye)

An art nouveau *bedroom*

(Drawing by Roger Banks-Pye)

More ideas for a kitchen

(Drawing by Roger Banks-Pye)

gramophone which would have been the latest craze in 1905. With all the fashionable enthusiasm for traditional and folk art, a Scandinavian painted wooden chest seemed appropriate: actually this is a modern toy made by Lundby, the Swedish firm, and included in their excellent range of dolls' house furniture. The colours had to be toned down a little, and the inside lined with a minutely-patterned end-paper, but with these minor alterations it fitted in perfectly.

Tiny brass candlesticks from a souvenir shop, with white birthday-cake candles, followed the 'simple life' pattern. The pictures, in plain wooden frames, are minute Kate Greenaway reproductions, and we are still looking for a tiny copy of G. F. Watts' *Hope* to set the final seal upon the décor.

Anyone concerned with education will find this sort of dolls' house is, in its own way, just as useful a teaching aid as the elaborate eighteenth-century models were. The specialised research needed before a period room can be begun provides an entertaining and painless way of studying social history, and a set of rooms ranging over say the past 300 years will easily absorb a whole class of children, or a group of adults, in a joint creative enterprise.

1970s Kitchen and Sitting-room
The main difference between furnishing a period dolls' house and a modern one is that in the first instance you are limited by historical fact, whereas in the second you can allow your imagination free rein.

It's well worth spending as much time and thought at the planning stage of a modern dolls' house as you would on a period one. After all, a modern dolls' house will probably live to be an antique one day, and you will want it to be an accurate representation of your time.

Unless you happen to be an interior designer, it's difficult to get an overall picture of contemporary style. Most homes, though excellent to refer to for domestic detail, have grown

105

with their owners through the years, and are therefore a mixture of many styles and their décor the result of chance, sentiment and impulse buying as much as fashion. So when planning the rooms of a dolls' house, it's as well to step outside your own surroundings and take a wider look at the current scene.

The furniture departments of large stores provide a great many ideas for colours and new trends. Trips to department stores and furniture showrooms can serve as fantastic exhibitions of all that is current in furniture design. In New York visit Altman's, Bloomingdales, or Lord and Taylor on Fifth Avenue—and take in the Metropolitan Museum of Art as well.

Make a mental note of the rooms you prefer in friends' houses, of what clever decorating ideas and unusual colour schemes they have used. Buy some of the many magazines devoted to home-making, and not only the English-language ones, but the excellent magazines published in France and Germany, all of which are invaluable as a source of inspiration and for their colour pictures which can be cut out and used in a dolls' house.

In our kitchen, page 104, the oven front, the dials of the cooking range, the tiled wall and the papered wall behind the white shelves are all taken from colour magazines, while magazines also supplied two pictures, the tiles behind the fireplace, several book jackets and the miniature periodicals for the sitting-room.

Your own home will influence you a great deal of course. In fact, you will most likely find that your dolls' house will reflect your personality just as your home does, and that you will find yourself choosing the sort of colours, ornaments and furnishings that you would choose for your house if you were a completely free agent. On the other hand, anyone who is reluctantly living in a small flat in town can allow their fancy to roam and model a dolls' house on a Southern colonial mansion—or a Scottish crofter's cottage.

Having decided to make, and having planned, a 1970-style kitchen and sitting-room, we had to find something to put these two rooms in. To show how effective and permanent even a cardboard house can be, we used a strong cardboard box, divided in two. If you use a cardboard box, you must use a really strong one, because a flimsy carton tends to buckle after papering, and then it not only looks ugly but is difficult to furnish—cupboards and fitments will not stand properly against the walls, chairs and tables will fall over. Once divided, each room measured 8 inches high, 12 inches wide and 7 inches deep, which, working to a scale of about 1 : 16, was near enough average room size.

A characteristic of modern houses is their wide picture windows, and so we made two large openings at the back of the box. The edges of the window frames were neatened with white masking tape, giving a depth to the surround, and acetate sheet made the window glass. We placed a country scene behind the kitchen window, and outside the upstairs window, a picture of sky with clouds.

Papering a room is a straightforward job. We used white cartridge paper to add light to the kitchen, and thin scarlet cardboard for the sitting-room, mainly because it needed a lot of colour to contrast with the kitchen, but also because we just happened to have the right amount of scarlet card to hand.

A kitchen presents more design problems than a sitting-room, because space has to be found for large items like the refrigerator, sink, work surfaces, cupboards, oven and dish washer. It's strange how all these gadgets have come to be thought of as necessities in most homes; the inanimate substitutes for batteries of servants in the Victorian dolls' houses.

We also wanted a kitchen desk (because we'd admired one illustrated in a magazine article and there was no room for one in our real-life kitchen), and a breakfast bar that wouldn't project too far into the room and thus hide things and hinder access to everything else. An additional

107

problem was that the fridge needed a lot of space in front of it to allow its door to open.

Several diagrams later, we managed to fit it all in, and after laying the tile floor (varnished brown card with squares drawn on it) we began to build the kitchen fitments. A real kitchen unit is about 34 inches high, so sticking to the 1:16 scale, we made fitments $2\frac{1}{4}$ inches high, cutting them and the ceiling cupboards from a cork tile. Cork is an easy material to work with. It cuts easily and is strong as well as being a nice colour. It would have been possible to fit opening doors, hinged on bits of ribbon, but instead we contented ourselves with drawing the doors on the fitments with black felt-nib pen. The working surfaces were cut from white cardboard, in which we had also housed the sink unit, which was a small white plastic butter container.

As soon as the kitchen had been completed this far, wanting to complete the structural building for both rooms at the same time, we built the shelves in the sitting-room out of balsa wood, and glued them in place on the back wall.

White plastic sink edging (left over from the fitting out of a real kitchen) made window sills, and the kitchen sill was furnished with small pot plants from a toy garden kit. The kitchen Venetian blind was made of strips of cardboard hung on cotton.

Having completed the structural work on the two rooms, it was time to get down to detail, first in the kitchen, then in the sitting-room.

An oven was the prime requirement for the kitchen. Had we been able to find a really up-to-date model in a toy shop, we would certainly have bought it, but all those we saw were at least twenty-five years behind the times, so instead we made one out of a small square cardboard box, cutting out a magazine photograph of an oven for the front. The dish washer is another cardboard box, painted white, and this opens to reveal a plastic inner basket containing dishes. We moved the cooking rings (silver foil on a black background) along the working surface at the side of the room to allow space for the fake oven door to pull down.

One thing leads to another, and if there are cooking rings in the centre of a working surface, there must be a chimney to get rid of the cooking fumes. Bricks give a room a cosy character and we made a wall with a chimney out of railway modeller's brick paper, which is expensive but worth it if you need only a small amount.

Realistic-looking pots and pans are difficult to make, and we also wanted a fridge with a proper door that would open and shut, so we bought these at a toy shop for a small sum, buying at the same time delightful scale models of a pop-up toaster, a box of knives and forks, a dinner service, small sieve, and electric mixer. These were all luxury items in that one is not forced to buy them in order to make a realistic kitchen, but they do add great charm and would all be almost impossible to make at home.

Our sitting-room buys were fewer, two chairs, a sofa, the telephone, a globe and a brass mug (the last two were keyring finds).

The kitchen writing desk (drawers drawn in with feltnib pen), the kitchen table, and the rolling pin were made of balsa wood. The sets of kitchen shelves were made of white cardboard, backed with bright orange paper from a magazine. Milk, meat and butter, canisters of sugar, bowls of fruit and loaves of bread are all things that make a kitchen look lived-in, and these came next.

Extra plates were also easily made out of painted buttons. A drying-up cloth was more difficult, because you don't often find fabric printed with a very small complete pattern, so this was painted in water-colour on a small scrap of nonfray white fabric.

Quite often what you make is determined by what you find, and into this category fall most of the other things in the room. A piece of aluminium tube with a bead stuck in one end turned into a spotlight, square tops of setting lotion

109

bottles begged from the hairdresser were set on balsa wood bases to make stools, a plastic lid became a washing-up tray, with its drying rack made of a plastic basket, which strange though it may sound, actually began life in a jar of Spanish olives!

A discarded pottery brooch minus its clip was a decorative tea tray, a small bead stuck on top of a large bead suggested the shape of a biscuit barrel, sugar and flour canisters once containing pepper and salt were souvenirs of an air trip to Europe, and an assortment of buttons and oddments gave an impression of the clutter that seems to accumulate on every kitchen shelf in every country in the world.

The sitting-room was slightly easier to plan because there were no fixtures to decide on and no booked space apart from the window. The overwhelmingly bright red walls did pose a few colour problems once they were in place. The room needed to be cooled down, so we found some neutral-coloured fur fabric for a carpet—a little deep in pile for a real carpet perhaps, but suitably luxurious.

As we have said previously, there are several ways of making curtains for a dolls' house. Thin dress material will hang quite well on its own, and this is what we used here, sewing the fabric on to the gold jump links used in jewellery making. These formed curtain rings which could then be threaded on to a plastic knitting needle curtain pole, stopped at each end with a bead.

There don't seem to be any rules about how a modern fireplace should look, so you can use your imagination to create something truly original. Ours is made from a matchbox, covered with brick paper. The matchbox drawer, pulled out and painted black inside, has lengths of toothpick stretched across it to form the grate. Over the fireplace is a triangular plastic bottle-top chimney.

Small coloured pictures like ours of a ship and a horse are not hard to find. Magazines are the best source of supply, but many postage stamps bear excellent, clear reproductions which make splendid wall decorations.

The most satisfactory way of making an old-fashioned maple frame is to cut it, in sections, from balsa or matchbox wood, mitring the corners properly and then staining or painting it, and this is what we have done. Another frame was cut out of thick cardboard, with beads stuck on which, when painted a suitable colour, represented moulding. A picture mounted on board will look like an unframed canvas, an impression which is enhanced if you actually paint the picture yourself. Our avant-garde unframed picture was hand painted in gouache on a piece of flat balsa board.

Television sets are items of modern furnishing that are becoming more and more revolutionary in design. Ours was based on one seen in an advertisement, interpreted as a white polystyrene ball mounted on a section of an electric light fitting. Its antennae are large map pins.

A transparent table seemed just right for this room. It's a little plastic box standing on four collar studs. The radiator was once a set of plastic drawer dividers (from a do-it-yourself shop) cut in two, while ornaments like the oil lamp, the elephant and the bell on the shelves are the result of a diligent search through various friends' bead boxes. Cushions are tiny squares and circles of plastic encased in thin fabric, and the plates and glasses on the shelves are borrowed from the dinner service.

This seemed to complete the sitting-room for the moment, but there is no end to the things that will be added. A hi-fi set to go under the shelf, more light fittings, a bigger and better flower arrangement, a small piece of embroidery and embroidery bag, toys lying around. The top of the plastic table could be turned into a collector's table to hold small shells, ornaments and curios.

APPENDIX: MINIATURE CRAFT SUPPLIERS

Although, as we have pointed out in this book, those objects that can be used as raw materials for miniatures are limited only by the imagination of the craftsperson, the suppliers listed below can be contacted for various woods, metals, and trimmings. Send for catalogues when possible, since they provide ideas as well as ordering information.

A & L Hobbicraft
50 Broadway, Box 7025
Asheville, N.C. 28802
Catalogue: $1.00

P. S. Andrews Co.
603 So. Main St.
St. Charles, Mo. 63301
Catalogue: $2.00

Architectural Model Supplies, Inc.
115D Bellam Blvd.
P.O. Box 3497
San Rafael, Calif. 94902
Catalogue: $1.00

Bob's Arts and Crafts
11880 No. Washington
Northglenn, Colo. 80233
Catalogue: $2.00

The Brookstone Co.
Peterborough, N.H. 03458
Catalogue: $1.00

Chestnut Hill Studio
Box 38
Churchville, N.Y. 14428
Catalogue: $1.00

Constantine's
2050 Eastchester Road
Bronx, N.Y. 10461
Catalogue: 50¢

Deft Wood Finishes
P.O. Box 3669, Dept. DHN
Torrance, Calif. 90510
Send SASE for catalogue

Dollhouse Factory
Box 456, 156 Main St.
Lebanon, N.J. 08833

Dollhouse Factory
P.O. Box 2232
Sunnyvale, Calif. 94087
Send SASE for catalogue

Dollhouses
16460 Wagon Wheel Drive
Riverside, Calif. 92506
Send SASE for catalogue

Edabub's Dollhouse
R.D. #1, Box 84B
Great Barrington, Mass. 01230
Catalogue: 50¢

Green Door Studios
517 E. Annapolis St.
St. Paul, Minn. 55118
Catalogue: 50¢

J. Hermes
Box 23
El Monte, Calif. 91734
Send SASE for catalogue

Holgate & Reynolds
601 Davis St.
Evanston, Ill. 60201
Catalogue: $1.00

The Lilliput Shop
5955 S.W. 179th Ave.
Beaverton, Ore. 97005
Catalogue: 50¢

Lilliput Unlimited
P.O. Box 450
La Mirada, Calif. 90637
Catalogue: 25¢

Metal Miniatures
601 Davis St.
Evanston, Ill. 60201
Catalogue: 25¢

The Miniature Mart
883 - 39th Ave.
San Francisco, Calif. 94121
Catalogue: $2.00

C. A. ("Chuck") Newland
2465 E. Commonwealth
Fullerton, Calif. 92631
Catalogue: 25¢

Northeastern Scale Models, Inc.
Box 425
Methuen, Mass. 01844
Catalogue: $1.00

Pickwick Miniatures
P.O. Box 297
Glenview, Ill. 60025
Catalogue: $1.00

Doreen Sinnett Designs
418 Santa Ana Ave.
Newport Beach, Calif. 92660
Catalogue: $1.00

Talents Unlimited
801 Glenbrook Road
Anchorage, Ky. 40223
Catalogue: $2.00

Walther's
4050 No. 34th St.
Milwaukee, Wis. 53216
Catalogue: $1.00

The Workshop
424 No. Broadview
Wichita, Kan. 67208
Catalogue: $1.00

Index

115

117

118

119